Hear Us Roar

AN ANTHOLOGY OF EMERGING WOMEN FOOTBALL WRITERS

Hear Us Roar

AN ANTHOLOGY OF EMERGING WOMEN FOOTBALL WRITERS

First published in 2023 by Fair Play Publishing
PO Box 4101, Balgowlah Heights, NSW 2093, Australia
www.fairplaypublishing.com.au

ISBN: 978-1-925914-62-7
ISBN: 978-1-925914-63-4 (ePub)
© Bonita Mersiades (compiler/editor) et al 2023

The moral rights of the authors to their individual contributions have been asserted.

All rights reserved. Except as permitted under the *Australian Copyright Act 1968* (for example, a fair dealing for the purposes of study, research, criticism or review), no part of this book may be reproduced, stored in a retrieval system, communicated or transmitted in any form or by any means without prior written permission from the Publisher.

Cover design and typesetting by Ana Secivanovic

Photographs are from the personal collections of the individual contributors, as well as Alamy, Syeda Mahpara Shahid and Joel Litsé.

All inquiries should be made to the Publisher via hello@fairplaypublishing.com.au

A catalogue record of this book is available from the National Library of Australia.

Other than a payment to each of the individual contributors, the proceeds of this book will be given to the Literacy for Life Foundation, an Aboriginal-led adult literacy organisation, and Future4Nepal, co-founded by Thomas Hitzlsperger to build a school and sporting facilities in a Nepalese village impacted by the building of facilities for Qatar 2022.

CONTENTS

Introduction 1

Players 3

Sissi: The Unsung Hero of Brazilian Women's Football 4
Keeping the Hope Alive: The Story of a Pakistani Goalkeeper 20
From Rejection to Stardom: The Lamine Mana Story 29

Developing Women's Football 39

The Development of Women's Football in Cameroon 40
Coconut Football: A Bittersweet Relationship 49
For Women Only: Unique Issues for Women in Football 56
The Shine of Women and Girls in Brazilian Soccer:
An Illustrated Story 63

Changing the Game 75

How Viktoria Berlin is Revolutionising Women's Football
in Germany 76
Boardroom to Bleachers:
Representation and Societal Issues in Football 87
Football Fandom 99
Virtual Turnstiles: Barriers to Entry and
Technological Gatekeeping in Women's Football 111
Racism in Women's Football 121

Fiction 131
Sidelines 132
Izzy's Magical Soccer Adventure 144

Personal Stories 163
My Love is for the Red, Red Rose 164
Three Goals That Changed Me 176
Football. Bloody Hell. 187
The Judging Panel 200

Introduction

The 17 stories that follow come from a global Emerging Women Writers' competition that I initiated as part of the 2023 Football Writers' Festival.

I have long been of the view that, in Australia at least, football could be in a better position than it is in comparison to the other sporting codes if only it was more accessible and more relevant to more women.

This is true, of course, in relation to participation and players from grassroots to elite level.

But advancing women in the game and being more relevant to them is not just about on-the-field endeavours. It is also what happens in football boardrooms and administration, and more broadly how women can be part of a football culture.

Media, journalism and writing are critical elements of developing a football culture, and girls and women deserve to be as much a part of football culture as boys and men.

As Australia was co-hosting the Women's Football World Cup in 2023, I thought an Emerging Women Writers' initiative would be a positive way for FIFA to demonstrate that it is truly committed to advancing women in all aspects of the game. I wrote to FIFA and the Local Organising Committee in November 2021 suggesting that they adopt the idea.

Sadly, they failed to respond, so I just went about doing it anyway.

The Emerging Women Writers' initiative was launched in September 2022 inviting women to submit a long-form article (between 3,000 and 5,000 words) related to football on any topic and of any genre. It was encouraging to receive entries from 16 countries that covered a wide range of topics and issues.

The articles selected for this anthology are written by women from 11 countries from every continent except – somewhat ironically but perhaps not surprisingly – Australia. Coincidentally, all of FIFA's six regional confederations are represented which just reinforces what so many of us know: that football is the most global of sports, it speaks a universal language, and can engage not just the interest, but the passion, of women as fans and writers.

In other words, football culture is for women too!

My thanks to Marcela Mora di Araujo (Argentina), Stephanie Brantz (Australia), Nick Harris (Scotland), Inas Mazhar (Egypt), Osasu Obayiuwana (Nigeria) and Laura Williamson (England) who, along with me, read, rated and ranked all entries to arrive at our 17 published articles.

Thank you also to the many women who submitted an entry. I encourage all of you – and those who may be reading this who also aspire to be a football writer - to keep observing, to keep asking questions, to keep holding individuals and organisations to account, to never lose interest, and to keep writing.

Bonita Mersiades
Sydney, Australia

Players

Sissi: The Unsung Hero of Brazilian Women's Football

by Olga Bagatini

How the first genius of Brazilian women's football, considered a legend by FIFA, was rejected for shaving her head and to this day lacks prestige and recognition in her own country.

The Brazilian team went from being the underdogs to the surprise packets at the 1999 FIFA Women's World Cup. Though discredited by their national press and undervalued by the governing body of Brazilian football (known as the CBF), the players pulled off an historic campaign.

The squad made its debut with a 7–1 win over Mexico, with three goals by Sissi. In the second match, the team beat Italy 2–0, with another two incredible goals scored by Brazil's No. 10. Against Germany, in another gala performance by the left-footed player, Brazil drew and qualified for the quarter-finals as group leaders.

In the quarter-finals against Nigeria, Brazil took a 3–0 lead, but lapses let Nigeria tie the score at 3–3 and take the game to overtime. The first team to score a golden goal would immediately win. After 20 tightly contested minutes, Brazil got a free kick on the left side of the field. Sissi picked up the ball and prepared herself for the kick.

"There was this blessed foul near the area," recalled Wilsinho Riça, who was head coach of the team in 1999. "Everyone expected Sissi would cross the ball into the box. Instead, she shot it straight into the top left corner, taking everyone by surprise, including the Nigerian goalkeeper. She scored."

Sissi ran across the field in celebration, roaring as she was embraced by her thrilled teammates. It was the best moment of her career, and an

PLAYERS

unprecedented moment for Brazilian women's football.

"Only someone with a high degree of technique, sensitivity and creativity could score a goal like that," added Wilsinho.

Brazil ended up losing in the semi-finals to the United States, who went on to win the tournament.

However, the Brazilian team beat Norway in the penalty shoot-out in the third-place play-off and returned from an official tournament with a medal for the first time.

Sissi scored seven goals and was the tournament's top scorer, alongside China's Sue Wen. As China reached the final, Wen was voted the FIFA World Player of The Year, with Sissi in second place. The Brazilian midfielder was invited to the FIFA gala to receive the Golden Boot and the Silver Ball awards in a moving ceremony attended only by world-class footballers.

"I was never much of a scorer; my thing was providing passes and assists, but the goals simply happened, one after the other," recalled Sissi. "What surprised me the most was the recognition I received during the tournament. I saw the crowded stadiums, the girls wearing banners with my name on them, the people asking me for autographs and pictures. And there was that incredible award ceremony."

In 2015, FIFA took votes to select the best goal in Women's World Cup history and showcased Sissi's goal against Nigeria among the finalists. With that free kick and her overall performance in 1999, Sissi wrote her name on the pages of World Cup history and paved the way for women's football to be treated with more respect in Brazil.

"I think I did all that because I wanted to prove to the Brazilian people that women could play football in a country where almost nobody accepted us," Sissi explained—she is the unsung hero of Brazilian women's football.

* * *

Beheaded dolls in Bahia

When Sisleide 'Sissi' Lima do Amor was born on June 2, 1967, women were lawfully forbidden to play football in Brazil. The law was enacted in April 1941 and stated that women would not be allowed to play sports "incompatible with their nature". In 1965, the law was made more specific, and sports such as football, wrestling, rugby and water polo were expressly prohibited for women because they were allegedly "unsuitable for the female body". This ban was not revoked until 1979. It caused a four-decade delay in developing women's football in Brazil and established stigmas and prejudices that still exist today.

However, even discrimination and the risk of arrest didn't prevent Sissi from falling in love with the sport that's considered an indelible mark of Brazilian national identity. Born in the small town of Esplanada in the state of Bahia, Sissi had football as one of the few leisure activities in her poverty-stricken childhood in one of the country's driest regions. She scored her first goals playing in the streets as the only girl among a bunch of boys. But they would not always allow her to play, claiming football was a boys-only sport. Her parents were not happy about her playing either. No matter how much she asked to be gifted a ball for Christmas, Sissi would only get dolls.

"I suffered prejudice; our neighbours said bad things about me to my parents and cursed at me for playing football. I felt deeply the discrimination caused by this law banning women's football. But I didn't care about that; I was always very rebellious, and I knew I would do anything to be able to play," Sissi explained.

Tired of not being taken seriously on the pitch, left-footed Sissi invented her own way to play using her home resources. At some point, she started ripping the heads off her dolls to have something round to kick. This may sound surprising now, but that was a widespread practice among female players from the 1960s, '70s and '80s who were not allowed to play with the boys.

Sissi's older sister, Lígia do Amor, was horrified by the beheaded dolls and had to hide her own toys from her younger sister. However, as time passed, Lígia understood Sissi's passion for football and began to use her influence as an older sister to persuade their parents to finally give Sissi a ball and allow her to play with the boys on the street.

Sissi's passion was better accepted when her family moved to a bigger town called Campo Formoso at the same time as the government lifted the women's football ban in 1979. There, Sissi had her first contact with other girls who played and she started participating in school tournaments. She stood out in the squad, which led to invitations to play in local amateur teams: first, Grêmio de Senhor do Bonfim, then Flamengo de Feira de Santana, which was considered the best squad in the region.

"She simply dominated the game in Bahia," said Solange Bastos, Sissi's former teammate in Flamengo de Feira and the national team. "She was the best on the pitch, always winning individual awards in the tournaments. We were just teenagers, but she had impressive skills with the ball."

Sissi gets her first big break

After playing for Flamengo de Feira for a few years, Sissi was invited to join Bahia Brahma in 1985. She was 17 when she moved to Salvador, the capital of Bahia, where she played both football and futsal. Like most women's teams at that time, Bahia Brahma was not linked to an official club. It was a personal project of a man called Faustino Silva, a women's football enthusiast. There was no remuneration for players, only a daily allowance to pay their bills in the capital. "We had an outstanding group, but there was no money involved. We did everything we did because of our love for football," said former player Rosana Fernandes, Sissi's teammate in Salvador.

In Bahia, Sissi nurtured the dream of becoming a professional player and moving to a larger city. The Brazilian women's football landscape was changing with the ban's end. Several amateur women's teams and tournaments were created, especially in the country's wealthiest cities, Rio de Janeiro and São Paulo. The most prominent team at the time was Radar from Rio. It emerged as a beach soccer team on Copacabana beach before it took the pitch, winning the state championship six times.

The global scene for women's football was under transformation as well. Under pressure from European players who demanded better structure and conditions for women's football, FIFA organised an international competition in 1988 to evaluate the feasibility of an official Women's World Cup. As a result, the FIFA Women's Invitation Tournament was held in China with 12 participants, including Brazil.

Having been a stand-out locally in Bahia, Sissi was invited to join the first official Brazil women's team in China alongside players from Rio who were considered stars, such as Roseli and Cebola who both played for Radar. Sissi joined her new teammates in Rio before heading to China. It was her first time on a plane.

However, the pioneering generation who represented Brazil in their first official women's team received little instruction and no support from football managers of the time.

The kits, for instance, were a big issue. The Brazilian Football Confederation (CBF) didn't bother ordering custom-made jerseys for the ladies, and the women received the leftovers of sports equipment men had worn in previous competitions. Thus, shorter female players needed to fold their shirts and sew their sleeves to fit. In addition, the CBF didn't send support staff such as a professional cook, as is customary nowadays. Faced with the distinctive Chinese cuisine, many players later said that during those weeks they primarily ate M&M's chocolates, as they were the tournament's sponsor.

Sissi scored a goal against Norway in the second match, leaving her first mark on the national team, but she was young and didn't play a central role in a squad filled with the Radar stars. Despite the adversities, Brazil finished the 1988 Invitation Tournament in third place. The competition's success led to FIFA's approval of the establishment of the first official Women's World Cup to also be held in China in 1991.

Upon returning from Asia, Sissi accepted an invitation to play for Corinthians, one of the most traditional clubs in São Paulo. However, in contrast to the success of the Invitation Tournament, there was yet another setback in the development of Brazilian women's football. Once again, the prominence of female athletes bothered the old-fashioned male managers who ran the sports organisations in Brazil. This time, the president of the São Paulo Football Federation, who had just been elected, announced that women would not be allowed to register as professional players in the State. As a result, the Federation went for years without fostering the sport or even organising official competitions. The situation in Rio de Janeiro was not much different. The Radar's president's death at the end of the 1980s led to the team's shutdown.

Suddenly, all the achievements in women's football in previous years went down the drain. From 1989 to 1994, female tournaments practically disappeared, except for a few sporadic editions. However, the weakening of women's football created the opportunity to strengthen the futsal scene, and new teams and competitions were established. Sissi played for several futsal teams in the early '90s, such as Bordon, Marvel, Sabesp and Euroexport, and won several titles and individual awards.

Unfortunately, an injury ruled her out of the first official Women's World Cup in 1991. Brazil, without adequate preparation and practically no local football competitions, did poorly, finishing in ninth place.

However, women's football began to resurface in Brazil in 1994, due to changes in the management boards of the leading football organisations and the prospect of the next World Cup in 1995. The CBF elected Romeu Castro—a true enthusiast of women's football—to lead a new development project for the women's national team. Romeu managed to negotiate unprecedented sponsorships and broadcasting rights for the women's matches, and he strengthened the fixture calendar to allow players to gain experience. Brazil easily earned a spot in the World Cup by winning the Copa América.

But there was even more at stake: the International Olympic Committee announced the introduction of women's football for the 1996 Olympics. The eight best-placed teams in the 1995 World Cup would be guaranteed an unprecedented Olympic spot.

Castro's measures, however, did not change the mentality of most of the sports managers of the time, who were still against giving better status to female footballers. Several players expressed the sexism and discrimination that they felt from those men who made little effort to improve the conditions of the women's game. Women also reported pressure to meet an "aesthetic standard of femininity", as the CBF believed this would be a critical factor in attracting a larger audience and more sponsors to women's football. Players who did not meet the standards of heteronormativity were forbidden to express their preferences in public.

Brazil didn't do well at the 1995 World Cup and were disqualified in the group stage, suffering a 6–1 defeat against Germany and ending up in ninth place. However, an off-field factor granted Brazil an Olympic qualification. England finished the World Cup in seventh place, but as the country could only participate in the Games as Team GB (Great Britain), their Olympic qualifying spot was given to the ninth-placed Brazil. So began another period of glory for women's football in the country.

Consolation prize

With a place in the Olympics secured, Brazil's National Olympic Committee joined the CBF in designating funds for the women's squad. This created a small revolution in their conditions. Prestigious manager José Duarte was hired to coach the ladies, bringing considerable positive publicity to the team. Duarte became a crucial figure in Sissi's development as a player. He insisted that Brazil's No. 10 wore the captain's armband, believing in her abilities to lead and inspire other players both on and off the pitch. Moreover, for the first time the jerseys were custom-made to fit the players' bodies.

Brazil made its Olympic debut with a draw against Norway and defeated Japan in the second match, giving the players significant self-confidence. Still, they had to at least draw with Germany in the last group-stage game to qualify. The 6–1 defeat by Germany in the 1995 World Cup was still stuck in the Brazilians' minds, and the Germans opened the scoring in the fourth minute. Nevertheless, with a beautiful goal by Sissi, Brazil equalised the score and qualified for the semi-finals, surprising everyone including the CBF. Not believing in the chances of the women's team's success, the CBF had bought the team's return flight tickets for the day after the group stage ended.

In the semi-finals against China, Brazil was winning 2–1 when Sissi suffered an ankle injury and had to leave the pitch. Without the star responsible for dictating the team's pace, Brazil suffered two goals against them in the final ten minutes and lost the match. Shaken by the defeat, the team went on to lose the bronze medal match against Norway, and as the CBF didn't have return flight tickets for the female players, the team's managers had to devise a creative solution to send the group back home.

"The solution was to book us on the charter flight reserved for the men's team, where there were stars like Ronaldo and Roberto Carlos," said former player Márcia Tafarel. "CBF still had the nerve to say it was our reward for reaching the final stage! The men's award was R$45,000 for each player, while our award was the *opportunity* to be on that flight with them... Absurd."

Brazil realises women can play football

The unforeseen success at the 1996 Olympics finally opened up space for creating a solid women's football league in São Paulo called 'Paulistana'. It was the first league with a professional structure in South America, and its matches were broadcast on TV. Sissi signed to play for São Paulo who were coached by José Duarte, and whom she saw as a father figure. He made her captain.

The team won 28 of their 32 games in 1996. They scored 199 goals, conceded only 22, and became both state and national champions. As the team's talisman, Sissi was responsible for many of those goals and began to be called "Empress Sissi" by sports commentators. That team is still to this day considered one of the best Brazil has ever seen, and its sensational performances led to a remarkable episode that showcased the potential of women's football to the public.

One night, frustrated with the frequent defeats of São Paulo men's squad, the fans improvised a joke rhyme in the packed stadium during a match: "Hey, Muricy, bring on Sissi! Hey, Muricy, bring on Sissi!". Muricy Ramalho was São Paulo's men's team's head coach—and that was the time a predominantly male crowd chanted a female player's name.

From 1996 to 1999, Sissi continued to rack up goals and was considered the country's best female player. With the gradual development of the Brazilian women's football leagues, the national team arrived well-trained and self-assured for the 1999 World Cup in the United States. It was in this context that Sissi's star shone once and for all; she gained global prominence, and her name went down in the history of women's football. She scored seven goals—including her marvellous goal against Nigeria.

"It was the best moment of my career," claimed Sissi.

The daring of a shaved head

During the 1999 World Cup, Sissi shaved her head because of a promise she had made to her teammate, Formiga. The decision inspired admiration in some and shock in others—especially from the CBF's male managers who insisted on linking female footballers with "femininity". Images of the skilful and shaved-headed player ran around the world and became Sissi's trademark during her outstanding performance in the World Cup.

"The acceptance among the public was fantastic. However, some people in CBF thought I was trying to cause controversy and shock people. It was ridiculous," said Sissi.

Yet, the shaved head was just one of Sissi's traits that caused discomfort in Brazil's old-fashioned football managers. They were also bothered by her sexual orientation. Sissi identifies as a lesbian.

"It was unacceptable to them; they used to say it was a disease. To acknowledge my preferences and lifestyle was unthinkable then," said Sissi. "We couldn't talk openly about it. Seriously, there was a time they even put some staff to spy on players. They came to our rooms to see what we were doing, who we were with... We were not free to be who we were."

Moreover, as a leader, Sissi always used her position to demand better salaries, awards, sponsorships and structure for women in football from CBF managers. At the end of the 1990s, female players were upset because one of the sporting manufacturers sponsored only the men's team. And yet, it was the same jersey for men and women. Women also provided brand visibility by wearing the sponsored kit during their matches but received none of the sponsorship money.

Led by Sissi, athletes orchestrated a protest during a game when they entered the pitch with a stripe covering the sponsor's name. Managers didn't appreciate the move. Overall, the men in charge of football in Brazil thought they were doing women a favour by letting them play the game and wear the prestigious Brazilian yellow jersey. They believed women should be more than satisfied with what they received.

"Our generation had to face sexist managers who didn't see women's football with good eyes. We didn't have much support or money, but we put our hearts out there. However, we were naive to think things would change if we communicated those issues to them," said former player Tafarel.

Athletes reported that the CBF found ways to retaliate against those who protested and demanded a better structure for women. The managers often tried to intervene in the call-up lists, pressuring coaches to leave players who weren't fitting their behaviour standards. But they couldn't send Sissi away as she was one of the world's best players.

"CBF only wanted the prettiest, the most feminine and well-behaved girls in the team. I'm sure many people didn't want Sissi there, but they had to suck it up, because how would they explain the absence of the national star if she was playing well in her club and wasn't injured? They simply had to accept her," stated Tafarel.

Despite pressure from the managers, Sissi was comfortable in her own skin and kept both her attitude and shaved head. Firstly because of her promise to Formiga, but later because upon arriving in the United States she received a request from a school to meet a 12-year-old boy named Julius who was bullied because a cancer treatment had made him bald. Sissi went to the school to show the other children that it was common—and even *cool*—to have a shaved head. That encounter was a life-changing moment for her. The boy died a year later, and she decided to keep her head shaved as a tribute to him.

Sissi left São Paulo in 2000 to play for Vasco in Rio de Janeiro. The club had a professional and an Under-17 team where another skilful left-footed player was emerging. Unlike Sissi, she played as a striker and used to score loads of goals in the youth team's friendly matches against the main squad, disconcerting older players with her dribbles. Her name was Marta.

"At the age of 14, it was clear she had a unique talent and was going to be outstanding," recalled former Vasco athlete Suzana Ferreira. "I remember we used to talk a lot to her, and Sissi offered advice about her career. They used to practise free kicks together."

Sissi left Vasco a few months later to play in the United States where a professional league was under development, and women's football was more respected. Unfortunately for sports enthusiasts, the two most skilful left-footed players in Brazilian women's football never had the chance to play together in an actual match.

The CBF finds a way to get rid of Sissi

While preparing for the Sydney 2000 Olympics, Sissi had a disciplinary issue with coach Wilsinho. She refused to follow his orders during a training session, but later they sorted it out. However, CBF managers later used that episode as one of the excuses to get rid of the rebel star who represented a threat to the values they wanted for women's football.

In addition, the team failed to repeat the excellent performance of the 1999 World Cup and finished the Sydney Games in fourth place. It was the last official tournament Sissi would ever play with the national team. After that, the CBF used the excuse that the squad would undergo restructuring and went years without calling her up, even though she was playing at a high level for the San Jose CyberRays in California.

Coach Wilsinho recognised that her absence from the lists was not a matter of performance. "Removing Sissi from the national team was more a form of revenge than a decision that made sense from a rational point of view because she was still capable of playing big tournaments," said the coach who left the national team after the fiasco at the Sydney Olympics.

Sissi also believed that her reputation made the CBF push her away. "I paid a high price for speaking out, for being who I was, but I don't regret it. I did what I thought was right," she claimed.

The most awkward situation Sissi would face was yet to come. Playing in California, she had already been left out of the 2003 World Cup squad. Brazil was beginning preparation for the 2004 Athens Olympics when Sissi received a call from head coach Renê Simões. He wanted to sound out her interest in returning to the national team. Sissi claimed she accepted immediately, but after a few days of not hearing any news, she decided to call him back. Then she heard that the coaching staff had held a meeting and decided it would be better if she didn't go.

At the time, Simões didn't give much of an explanation to Sissi. But years later, he gave his version of the facts. The former head coach claimed the coaching staff weren't sure about her physical and technical condition after so many years away. There were also concerns about her relationship with the group because of her past disciplinary issue and prolonged absence. So, it was decided it was better to leave her out. The situation was never properly clarified by the CBF.

"The sorrow I felt with this story took a long time to heal. After all those years playing for the national team, representing Brazil in the best way possible, they simply said, 'Your story ends here.' I didn't even get the closure I deserved. I stopped caring about the Brazilian team; for a long time, I didn't want to see the matches. It was the most difficult moment of my life," recalled Sissi.

The main character of the 1999 World Cup was treated as persona non grata by football's governing body in Brazil.

"She really went out through the back door," explained Brazilian sports researcher Edson de Lima.

And so, the first great genius of Brazilian women's football was forced to retire from the national team without any tributes or a proper farewell.

Honours, tributes and recognition

Frustrated with her omission from the Athens Olympics squad in 2004, Sissi began studying to become a coach. She retired as a player in 2009 and has been working as a coach of young girls' teams in California ever since, helping to develop new talent in women's football.

At a global level, she is literally considered a legend.

Sissi is part of a select list of former players called the "FIFA Legends". They are regarded as the best footballers of all time. This title gives her a chance to participate in several FIFA events where she uses her voice to raise awareness of the need for better conditions for women's football in Brazil.

She is popular in the United States too. Several world-class American female footballers, such as Megan Rapinoe, have spoken about how

Sissi inspired them. Her story was depicted in Chelsea Clinton's book *She Persisted Around the World: 13 Women Who Changed History* (2018) alongside other brilliant women like Malala Yousafzai. Brazil's former No. 10 also appears in the International Football Hall of Fame in Mexico. In 2022, FIFA launched a documentary about her life and career.

Despite being one of the greatest players in Brazilian women's football history and recognised as such worldwide, Sissi isn't properly recognised in her own country. With her abrupt departure from the national team and the lack of effort by both the CBF and traditional sports media to rescue and tell the stories of women in football, she spent years ostracised in Brazil. To this day, Sissi and other players from the pioneering generation are little known to the public—even to big football fans.

Made invisible for years, Sissi only began to have her accomplishments recognised in Brazil following the recent growth of women's football. In the wake of the success of the 2019 World Cup in France, Sissi has been contacted more often by the sports media to share her story and impressions about the current women's football stage. Thus, her trajectory is progressively reaching a larger audience—but her public recognition is still far from matching up to her achievements.

There is currently a movement in Brazil led by independent sports journalists and women's football activists to pressure the CBF to improve their acknowledgement of both Sissi and the pioneering generation of female footballers. However, it is challenging to rescue these stories because the CBF has not preserved many documents, records and items from the early days of women's football.

In the CBF Museum for instance, there is astonishingly no mention of Sissi's and her generation's accomplishments, and thus no official record of how many goals she scored for the national team over the years. So those interested in learning about the history of women's football in Brazil need to rely on a few old newspapers—but mainly on the memories and stories told by the characters who lived that time.

The lack of recognition by CBF, the media and even by younger generations of female players is a resentment Sissi still carries with her. She would like Brazil's current female stars to better value the players of the past who paved the way for them, just as men do—For instance, Richarlison always makes public statements of his admiration for Ronaldo.

Women like Sissi who defied adversity were discriminated against for daring to play as themselves and helped to put Brazilian women's football on the map. They deserve to have their stories told.

"I wish I could have the same respect in my homeland that I have globally. Maybe things will get better now since people have more opportunities to learn about my story and the stories of the other pioneering female players," said Sissi.

"Deep down, I just want to be remembered for everything I did in football, so my story can leave a positive legacy for the next generations of players."

Olga Bagatini is a Brazilian journalist and an activist for the greater participation of women in all areas of sport. Currently, she works at UN Women on a project that uses sport as a tool to empower girls from favelas (poor neighbourhoods). She has been researching the story of Sissi and the pioneering generation of Brazilian female players in recent years. Olga wants to write about them to bring these stories to a larger audience so that these women receive the recognition they deserve.

Keeping the Hope Alive:
The Story of a Pakistani Goalkeeper

by Natasha Raheel

"No one knows who [the real] Mahpara is, but everyone knows who Mahpara is—everyone knows Mahpara the goalkeeper, the footballer; whatever identity I had been able to carve, it has been because of the beautiful game," reflected Pakistan's former national team goalkeeper, Syeda Mahpara Shahid.

Carving an identity for oneself is the best pathway one can find to build a life, especially for the girls brought up in a country like Pakistan—where being a woman often is not enough of an identity on its own—it is more about whose daughter, sister or wife she is.

If you were to meet Mahpara, you would never guess what a fireball she is on the field. Outside the pitch she is a soft-spoken, often bubbly, quintessentially eastern, Muslim girl; but on the field, she can shout out to her entire team and lay down their international duties from the goalpost.

But mostly she is beautiful: inside and out.

Like many other footballers she suffered at the hands of the institutional crisis at the Pakistan Football Federation (PFF) where the girls last played their international tournament in 2014 before making a comeback in 2022 at the South Asian Football Federation (SAFF) Championship in Nepal.

The time that lapsed between 2014 and 2022 was a long and a hard eight years for all the footballers in the country, but for women more so. For them, just getting access to the playing field is a greater challenge than it is for men. Getting permission from family is another issue. Then to withstand the fact that the national Federation has not only been marred by political power-play and in-fighting between officials, but also by two FIFA suspensions

since 2014 (in 2017 and again in 2021) for third-party-interventions—all of these events only left Pakistan's women footballers more vulnerable than most. The path was not leading them to where they wanted to go.

The PFF had been dominated by political figures who wanted to stay in office. There were legal battles and multiple visits by FIFA delegations to assess the situation, leading to the world body appointing a "normalisation committee" in 2019 which again saw several changes in the PFF leadership.

Breaking barriers is not enough, and "breaking stereotypes" sounds even more clichéd than it is in times when the right to just play is often denied.

Mahpara, 29, was one of the original women's players who made their international debut along with the Pakistan team back in 2010 in the SAFF Championship.

Mahpara and her teammates were pioneers because they were the first ones to wear the Pakistan national colours on the international stage, and while the journey should have offered them more recognition and opportunities, they faced the misogynistic attitude from the Federation that mostly used women's football as a formality; more of a "tick-box" activity rather than an avenue to sincerely build a strong national side.

Mahpara played for her motherland, but more so, she played for her mother.

"It was always my mother, I played this game for her because she wanted to see me as a footballer," explained Mahpara as we spoke. She was making her comeback with the SAFF Championship in 2022.

"I look back and all I know is that she inspired me in so many ways. If she never pushed me to play football, I may have never looked at it at all. I was always interested in playing sports during my younger years, in my school and college I played volleyball, netball, handball, basketball, but never football really, in fact there was not much exposure to football in my early years, because in the school and colleges here in Pakistan they only take sports as a casual physical activity, nothing is taken seriously and so it was never something that was ingrained to be pursued professionally.

"But it all changed when my friends asked me to join them when they began playing football at this local club called the Young Rising Stars Club, and at that point my mother played the most crucial role—she told me to give it a shot, and my father had always taught me to commit to the things I do completely.

"I never do anything half-heartedly or without dedication, because, well that does not align with the values my father instilled in me, so I began taking it seriously, I had always been ambitious and competitive, so that played a huge role in learning everything quickly too, I suppose. So that was a start to this beautiful journey.

"I fell in love with football slowly but surely It has become a part of my identity in so many ways that I cannot really leave it behind, ever."

As Mahpara reminisced on her beginning in the sport, we spoke about what kept her going during the darkest and the longest nights for the women footballers in the country between 2014 and 2022. During that time, they did not play any quality tournaments locally as there had never been a structured calendar of events. They only ever got to play the annual Pakistan National Championships over a period of a few weeks each year, and then they were not able to play more.

Mahpara comes from the capital of the country, Islamabad. She made her way to the top because of the most crucial decision she ever made—she switched from being a defender to a goalkeeper. It was an unusual choice for a new player as most girls were only interested in becoming strikers or defenders.

It was a bold (or even naïve) move at the time because there was a dearth of quality goalkeeping coaches across the board in Pakistan—not just for women's game—but also for the men's.

In Pakistan, traditionally the goalkeeping job goes to the player who is taller or bigger in size. It is a primitive approach to appointing the position in modern football, but that was how the coaches and the trainers usually rolled the dice for the players.

"I chose football and goalkeeping became something I liked. It was an advantageous position to play I thought, it was a unique place. Back when I was still young, playing with my local club, with my coach Shahid, he really helped us. I found out that the club was making two teams—a junior team, and a senior team. He was the one who taught us how to touch the football, the rules and everything.

"I naturally chose to participate in the try-outs for the senior team because I felt I always had the hunger to do better and go bigger—and I got selected. This was exceedingly early on and then we found out there are try-outs for the national team, so we went in those too, and I got picked for the side! It was the biggest moment for me, and I really thought [about] my mother at the time too."

In a society where girls are not given the basic right to play freely in safe places even as children, Mahpara appreciates that her family has been her backbone.

"My family gets more excited than me each time my name is there in the list of players for the national side.

"In the beginning when I used to play sports, my brother used to worry a lot about me getting injured or breaking my bones, but then slowly he understood that I love sports," explained Mahpara.

Keeping hope is a survival strategy

Mahpara has always kept her football ambition and hunger alive whether she is playing at club level, for the national side, or for her departmental team WAPDA (the government institute responsible for water and power distribution).

In her national career so far, she has lifted the trophy as a champion six times, despite the irreparable damage during the eight years lost due to the PFF crisis.

"I played football early on after the 2015 crisis with the PFF. I went to play club football in Maldives. Then in UAE, I played for Rossoneri FC. Even though they were smaller tournaments, I gave them my all as well, but then one starts to lose hope if things would improve.

"I remember after 2018 I felt there was such hopelessness, we didn't know what else we can do," said Mahpara, although with Rossoneri FC she played against Arsenal Women FC in Dubai.

Staying positive has been a huge battle for her, like many other players.

"I remain[ed] positive because my coach Shahid, in the beginning ingrained it in us that we stay focused on our mental health, like losing and winning is a part of the sport; secondly, we try to focus on where we can improve ourselves, because at times blaming others is easy.

"I kept myself optimistic by making sure that my mental health is not affected by the game, by keeping our discipline. I feel if we live with discipline then that helps, it gives us the perspective that the game is one thing—but being a responsible human is another. Similarly, I find competitiveness, or even envy, to be a driving force too.

"We can totally turn these negative emotions into something productive and a force to drive us, because that way I can get that drive. I get to learn from other players. Like I am a goalkeeper and there are other goalkeepers too who may be better than me, but I use my feeling[s] to learn, to improve, but at the same time I keep it in mind to be kind. That is to keep my mind positive, that even in the worst of situations, we can spin it around.

"Like if my name is not on the list anymore, my process is: what did I not do to be eligible for selection, what is it that I can do to improve? I find myself driven through these ways, that we must move on, no matter what," said Mahpara.

Finding comfort in helping others

After we spoke for a while, Mahpara said that one of her ways to keep busy was to make another career as a fitness trainer.

I asked her how much she has changed from the girl who played for the national team in 2014 to the girl playing now. Her reply was profound and full of hope. She pivoted to being a personal trainer during that time.

"Eight years is a long time, and I feel after 2018 I lost hope, and at that time my only goal was to keep myself physically fit. If you had asked me this at that time, I would have told you that I was depressed, that I was not feeling good, but I just focused on keeping moving, staying fit, if anything.

"I used to think, if suddenly FIFA lifted the ban and if they make a team, I should at least be in a position to play, so I just put my mind to being fit. From that point I suppose it all took off, I really got into this [fitness training] and made a career too, because I found clients, women who needed help. I forgot about football during these few years, because I started to get these opportunities to spend productive time with women," said Mahpara, who suddenly did get into the national side in 2022 just a few weeks after FIFA lifted its almost 15-month-long ban that began in 2021.

"I was not into this field of fitness when I used to play football, but then I got work as a trainer, and usually if we play football we hear things like, 'you are 29, it is too old', but I made a good decision—I started working with clients and I stayed fit and healthy too, because it is of course like, you do not want to get hair treatment from a person that is bald, so of course why would anyone what to hire me as a fitness trainer if I am not fit myself? So that is something that gave me another way to experience life, and it showed me that we can overcome bad situations too. If I did not stay in this fitness training as a profession, I guess I would have lost everything.

"The thing is I didn't face much difficulty in coming back to the national side too. I know there are newer players, and yes eight years of our lives have gone to waste, lots of our sacrifices have not been recognised, but I still feel that age is just a number, and it all gives me so much joy, whether I play football or not, but just working with women on their fitness makes me feel I have done something good in life," explained Mahpara.

However, now being back in the game, she looks at the level of goalkeeping in South Asian countries and feels that there is not a lot of improvement in the standard since before Pakistan's eight-year break.

"I think the region can improve further. The techniques employed are the same, but of course when we look at the European game the change has been drastic and it is so much more competitive, but in goalkeeping alone we need to work on the techniques and learn more," said Mahpara, whose all-time favourite goalkeepers are former US player Hope Solo and Germany's Manuel Neuer.

Mahpara's journey reflects the balance that is the modern Pakistani woman—living on her own terms in a society that is dictated by the men running it.

Looking at the Pakistani women's game, Mahpara's story is a vignette on what Pakistani society is like. It's where gender-based violence against women is endemic. In fact, according to The Express Tribune in October

2022: "In the year 2019 alone, 25,389 incidents against women were reported, while in 2020, 23,789 cases of abuse and other crimes, including rape, came to the fore. Similarly, in 2021, 14,189 cases were registered." Research published in the International Journal of Peace paints a similar picture" "Pakistan has a population of over 229 million and was ranked as the fourth most dangerous country for women in 2021." Choosing the career of a footballer is more of a brave cause than just about any other profession for a Pakistani woman.

Mahpara feels that her personal heroes, the people who inspire her, are the everyday working women who go out of their homes to make a living for their families.

"I think my heroes are just women who go out doing their jobs. You are a woman, I am a woman, we are all getting out to support our families. I see my mother as my biggest inspiration who stood up for her family, she has to go out and work, or work in our home; there are lots of my friends who go out to work, and you know how people look at the women who work—they feel that they can treat us any which way they like, they feel they can mistreat us. But I think for women to just exist and stand for their families makes them my heroes. That is where I get my inspiration from, that is what we are proud about I think," said Mahpara.

But on the other hand, she touched upon the fact that as she is getting wiser, it is her family and mental health that has become her priority.

"I must say that I had not spent much time with my family because I was always playing, [and] travelling for football. But now I do, I find peace in the moments with my family. I feel that is how I want to make a difference too. Even if my name comes up on the selection list or not, I missed the camp in 2021, which was the first camp for us, even though we were not playing any tournament after it—I missed it because I wanted to stay with my father who had gone through surgery, so it just gave me the best perspective I feel," Mahpara explained.

She did not make selection for the national team in 2023 despite being a hard-working player. Even though there have been reports of emotional abuse and mental stress from the team's current coach Adil Rizki, Mahpara's journey continues as she finds younger girls who she can inspire to play football, and she trains women to be in their best shape.

Natasha Raheel is a Pakistani journalist covering major events in football, combat sports, Olympics sports and the like for The Express Tribune, Pakistan's daily English language newspaper. Her focus is women's sports, sports federations and development, but she has a personal connection to football as her late father loved the sport and taught her how to play. She would like to see more women get involved in sports journalism.

From Rejection to Stardom: The Lamine Mana Story

by Cassandra Kimaka

A few years ago, Lamine Mana was rejected by her family and community because of her passion to play football.

The prodigy had decided to abandon Koranic School. She resisted Muslim tradition to pursue a career in football with hopes of reaching unprecedented future heights.

Today, Lamine Mana has gone from being an outcast to becoming a leading role model for young, ambitious Muslims girls especially, as well as other professionals in the football industry in Cameroon.

She owes her rise to prominence to the support of her father. He was a fervent promoter of football who often organised competitions among the youth in a locality where the sport was largely uncommon. This was where the young Mana took her first steps with the ball.

But sadly, her father died in late 2019 when she was in her early teens.

In an exclusive interview, Lamine admitted that her father "knew he was dying". Before his death, he made her promise that she would not give up on football, regardless of the circumstances. She was also made to promise that she would look after the family and provide for them after his death.

Today, she plays for the Cameroon national team and with second division French side, Saint-Malo.

Mana revealed that it has been a long and uneasy fight to achieve her dreams of playing professional football. She had to brave the odds and prove doubters wrong—especially in a region where negative cultural practices relegated women to the background.

After losing her dad, the young Muslim girl confessed that her family were less supportive; her mum was reluctant to support her dreams and she was unwelcome in her neighbourhood. Many considered her as a failed child and often used her as an example that other girls shouldn't copy.

Lack of education and early marriages are still very common in some parts of the north region of Cameroon. Lamine says she refused to succumb to tradition and was hell-bent on playing football at the highest level.

It didn't take her long to finish as the most valued player (MVP) of the Cameroon women's top tier championship and score a record 19 goals and be credited with 4 assists.

Lamine is also one of the few players who has featured in all levels of Cameroon national female teams from underage through to senior level.

Difficult beginnings

Lamine Mana suffered from the contrasting views of her parents. While her father hoped to see her evolve into a world class superstar, her mother was focused on the path of Koranic education and marriage for her.

Mana started playing when she was a nine-year-old. Back then she didn't even have shoes to play in but she was still way better than the boys even with her bare feet.

"My Mum wanted me to go to Koranic school but after school I used to play around with my male friends and neighbours. Since we knew one another in my community, people who saw me play would report me to my mother and ask why she let me play football with boys."

Mana's mother, Haua Sani, restricted her from playing football in fear that she would start behaving like a boy.

"She did not wear dresses like a Muslim girl. She preferred trousers and shorts, and she had fun playing around with boys—instead of playing with dolls or female neighbours," Sani revealed.

Contrary to her mother, Lamine's father saw her potential. He supported Manchester United and wanted to see her play for the club he adored.

When she was still in primary school, she was a member of the team that represented her school at the FENASCO League B games. It's a competition organised by the National Federation of School Sports of Cameroon, known by the French acronym of FNSSC.

Each year, this competition groups thousands of children from different primary schools of the 10 regions in Cameroon who test their capacities in different sports like football, volleyball, handball and athletics. The aims are to promote physical education and discover young talent.

Eventually, Lamine made her mark. "Dada" (as her parents call her) rose to notoriety during Cameroon's National Youth Games (Dixiades) where she was the youngest player.

Thanks to her performance, she was closely followed up by a local club given that the Games were an opportunity to identify kids with potential. Lamine was called to play for Renaissance Women de Guider, a first division local club in the national championship found in the North Region.

During her matches she was spotted by the president of Amazones FAP, at the time arguably the most famous club in Cameroon with enormous talents and resources. She therefore had to move from Guider to Yaoundé. But her mother was against this.

"After my father's death I stopped [playing in] the championship but little did I know that I was wanted by Amazones FAP. The president called me regularly to ensure that I was fine, but also to convince me to play for his club. I told my mother, who prohibited me to go—I understood that she was still under the shock of my father's loss."

But on a fateful day, Lamine's mother eventually gave her blessing for Lamine to travel to pursue her dream. It's a moment she recounted with emotion.

"I was in the sitting room when my mother told me, 'Lamine I'm sorry I didn't let you go earlier, I don't have anything to give but I will pray for you so that you go as far as possible. Go and play.'"

The future member of Amazones FAP hurriedly called the club's president who spoke with her mother. The next day, Lamine Mana was on her way to Yaoundé, Cameroon's political capital, to make a big step toward becoming a renowned professional footballer.

A continuous fight

The story of Lamine Mana is not an isolated one in Cameroon. Others have more troubling stories to tell.

Raissa Yawoudou, another Muslim girl, admitted that her future was uncertain. Just like it was in Lamine Mana's case, it was inconceivable for Raissa's mother that her child could play football. She considered it an all-male sport. Raissa had siblings engaged in football and explained the method she used to join her brothers and enjoy her passion:

"When my brothers left to play, I [would] wait a moment, then dress like a normal Muslim girl, throw my sporting shoes over the fence and wear them once I was out."

Her relentless efforts to escape pushed her mum to accept that she wanted to play. "At a point in time, my mother [eventually] supported me, especially when I was selected for the FENASCO League B games."

When Raissa was in form one class (grade six), her club chose her to lead the female football team at their games—so did her primary school. She found herself in a dilemma to the extent that the principal of her school threatened to dismiss her.

Despite the warnings and with the support of her mum, she chose to play with her primary school mates. Her team won the competition and she was the leading goal scorer.

An example for Muslim girls

Lamine Mana has influenced many Muslims girls like Raissa Yawoudou. Both footballers originate from the North Region of Cameroon, a region predominantly dominated by Muslims.

There a Muslim girl is usually expected to attend school and get married early—and not practise football which is largely reserved for boys. Both women had difficulties in convincing family and others that they had a passion for football.

Raissa and Lamine both took part in the FENASCO League B games where they produced good performances which were a springboard to join local club, Renaissance Women de Guider. This led to the school dropout of both youngsters at the level of lower sixth (ninth grade) to enable them to play in the Guinness Super League, the national female football championship organised every year by the Cameroon Football Federation, FECAFOOT. The tournament has existed since 2008 and is sponsored by the brewery giant, Guinness.

Raissa had the opportunity to play with Lamine Mana at Renaissance Women de Guider before Lamine moved to Yaounde to join Amazones FAP. Lamine remains Raissa's role model and she would like to follow in her footsteps.

"It's true we played together in Guider but today she is in France and plays for the national team. It is the dream of every professional footballer to serve her country and play for a big club. At my level, I still have much to do to reach her performances. When I recover from my injury, I will have to double my efforts."

Lamine has undoubtedly rekindled hope in other young Muslims girls. She is showing that religion and cultural background are not hindrances to producing excellent results and becoming a footballer. Lamine expresses her gratitude to her fans who call her regularly to encourage her. "Sometimes, I receive calls from my elder sisters in the profession who tell me, 'Lamine, we appreciate what you do, how can we become like you?'"

The 2017 MVP disclosed her despair for the unveiled talents who do not have the opportunity to follow their dreams like she did. "We have talents in the Northern Region, but families do not admit that girls leave their land to play."

The 17-year-old footballer said she is happy with her performances so far but she has bigger objectives like playing for French club Paris Saint-Germain (PSG), as well as defending the colours of Cameroon at the Women's World Cup and other international competitions.

"My dream team is PSG and I believe I can join the team. If I double my efforts, I'm convinced I may sign a professional contract and contribute at my level to the development of football in my region of origin."

It is not only Lamine who inspires young Muslim girls in Cameroon, so do those who are already professionals. In a few years, more female Muslims may become professionals like Nchout Adjara, the 30-year-old member of the Cameroon national team who was nominated for the Confederation of African Football (CAF) Women's Footballer of the Year award in 2022.

Evolution in clubs

Lamine Mana has played for three clubs and affirmed that her time at each club has contributed to her evolution and performance. She explained that on arrival at Amazones FAP, she did not have enough time playing because more experienced professionals were always selected—a situation she knew she would face due to her young age.

"I knew I {would] not arrive and play the first matches; I was very young and professionals were put first. During the first season, I did not play any [first leg] encounter but I told myself that if I work hard, I will be able to become a major team member and make the professionals become substitutes."

During the second leg of the matches, she had some minutes on the pitch. "Toward the end of the championship, I played for 10, 20, 24 minutes. On the last three days, I was among the first 11 squad because I was replacing a player who was signing another contract."

The following season, she stayed with Amazones FAP. Three days before the start of the championship, she was named to start in a friendly match. "When the coach asked me to begin the encounter, I did not think twice. I gave everything, though it was friendly. From that moment I was on the starting list from the beginning to the end of the championship. The only moment I did not play was when I was absent, and that year I was the best player. I had 19 goals and 4 assists."

These statistics generated interest in the then 17-year-old player from numerous clubs. In a bid to step up her performance, she decided to play for one of the best clubs of the championship, AS AWA FC, the following season.

"I could not leave a club where I performed well for a smaller team. If this team happened to be defeated by my previous club, then I would have made the wrong choice. At AS AWA we really worked, the coached wanted the best from us and we followed the rhythm. To warm up for example, we used to run 2 km. The difference between AS AWA and my previous team [was] that at AWA it was more physical because we ran a lot; meanwhile at Amazones it was more tactical. At the beginning it was not easy, but I ended up adapting."

While playing for AS AWA FC, the MVP was called up by the Cameroon Under 20 national team.

"In my evolution in clubs, I thank coach Hassan Balla because he always had confidence in me. I remember when I sustained a hand injury and I stayed two to three weeks without playing. When I returned to the club, coach Hassan asked if I could play. I said, 'Yes, but I cannot begin the encounter.' Fortunately for me, he put me [on] at the beginning of the match and I scored three goals against Eding Sport de Lekie. At the end of the game, I just thanked him."

Aside from hard work, the midfielder underlined that teamwork and connection were aspects that she appreciated in the team that made her talent grow: "At AS AWA, we were a family. The problems of one person concerned everyone."

New president, better conditions

According to Lamine Mana, the accession of Samuel Eto'o, ex-international footballer and member of the male national team, to become the head of the Cameroon Football Federation in December 2021 has improved football in general—and women's football in particular.

"Before 2021, the winners of the championship just obtained a trophy and that was only for the champion. Second and third places received nothing. We had no bonus. In 2022, it [was] FC AWA who won and they obtained a cheque for 20 million CFA francs. We clearly see a change. I really thank him for that because he gives hope to the youth to have a salary at the end of the month and an encouragement for efforts."

In effect, the five best teams of the championship now share 50 million CFA francs. That is 20 million for the champion, 15 million for the runners-up, 10 million for third, 3 million for fourth and 2 million for the fifth-best club.

Lamine also appreciates the visibility female footballers now have thanks to the presence of cameramen and photographers in the stadium. It showcases their performances to clubs who may require their services.

"Today, you will see more and more camera professionals in the stadium; they capture our movements and exploits which we can use to show a club. Most times when a club wants your services, they ask for videos to evaluate you and see your performances. At first, we had no way to prove our qualities. Apart from providing this proof to clubs, they help you 'go viral'. You know if someone puts a video of you scoring on the internet, people will want to know who you are and will follow the championship. These are innovations which we appreciate, and they give hope that female professional football is gradually picking up."

After his election, FECAFOOT's president Samuel Eto'o created an online television channel called FECAFOOT TV. The channel broadcasts the activities of the different national teams, key moments of championship encounters (male or female) and of course the activities of the Federation.

Football and religion quite easy to manage

For Lamine and Raissa, football and religion are two passions that do not collide, but they are both necessary in their development. Lamine explained that she follows a stable schedule to not let one overcome the other: "When I am with the national team, we train twice a day at 6am and 3:30 pm. It gives me enough time to carry out the 5:30am prayer. By 12:50, I conduct another prayer after resting. Given that the next training session is at 3:30pm, I pray by 3pm. My next devotion is at 6:30 pm before dinner and after that is at 7:30pm. I respect a program [where] they enable me to pray five times a day, as my religion demands."

Raissa follows the same schedule with a few exceptions as she has not yet been selected for the national team. She has adapted her prayer sessions to the training and playing schedule that she follows with her club.

"During the championship, we train and play more matches so I adjust my timetable, but I always do the first prayer and the last."

Both players admitted that they observe fasting periods during Ramadan as demanded by their religion. Raissa recalled that when she was younger she used to tie a hijab (an Islamic cloth that covers the hair). According to her, this was a way to show her attachment to her faith and to respect its traditions.

"When I started playing, people thought I didn't respect the customs. To prove them wrong, I would dress up with my fabric or a burka boot on my boots and add my hijab. I did everything to look like a normal Muslim girl with the exception that I played football with boys."

Cassandra Kimaka of Cameroon is an undergraduate student at the Advanced School of Mass Communication in Yaoundé. She decided journalism was her passion in 2018 while undertaking work experience for Cameroon Radio Television. She has a particular passion for sport, including both women's and men's football.

Developing Women's Football

The Development of Women's Football in Cameroon

by Chansiline Nanze

The little ball girl with big dreams

In a small three-bedroom flat behind the MTN Stadium in Mbouda in the West Region of Cameroon lives 10-year-old Fleurette Lorraine Pelame Zime. Her dreams go beyond those of most children her age.

Fleurette wants to become the Nchout Njoya Ajara of her generation. Ajara, who is a Cameroonian professional footballer, plays for Serie A side Inter Milan and the Cameroon senior women's national team, known as the 'Indomitable Lionesses'.

In Mbouda, most girls her age spend their spare time helping their parents on the farm or selling with them in the markets—but not Fleurette. She would rather be playing football when she is not being a ball girl on a match day of the MTV Elite One Championship.

Born as a twin to a family of five, Fleurette hasn't had life very easy. Firstly, she, her siblings and mother, Fokou Armande, were abandoned by her dad and she spent the first years of her life without experiencing the love of a father. Fokou Armande added that "He abandoned me for a richer woman when I gave birth to Fleurette and her twin brother. I was in Limbe by then. The little earnings from my roast fish business could not sustain myself and five kids. So I had no choice but to relocate to Mbouda where I could farm. Fortunately I met an old friend, Ngepi Vougue Yves Blériot. He took us in and became the father of my children. He is the one who suggested that we register my daughter in football school."

In an African context, it is difficult to have a man accept a woman with five kids from a previous relationship and take total responsibility for them.

So Fleurette is considered fortunate.

"Her foster father and I noticed she has a keen interest in football each time we are watching a game at home. She is always keen to copy the actions of players and she also likes playing with her brothers. She also plays in her school's team. So we decided to enrol her in the football academy," said Fleurette's mother.

Fleurette now trains with the African Future Stars Academy, a local football school based in Mbouda. It is the only one in her locality, and it is not well-equipped so she has to make do with its substandard training tools. For Fleurette, the most important thing is acquiring skills.

The year five primary school students have a weekly Saturday training session, increasing to three to four sessions each week during the school holidays. Fleurette's coach and the promoter of the African Future Stars Academy, Eudes Djockeng, told me that "Our program has been designed to ensure that the education of the pupils is not interrupted. That is why we hold our sessions every Saturday morning. Generally, we work for an hour, at most two, because they are still children and we cannot overwork them."

He added that: "As of now, Fleurette is the only girl training at the academy. She is the only female to have passed our test. Here we take the academic performance of the child into consideration before admitting. While we want to develop football talents, we also encourage mainstream education.

"What impressed me with Fleurette during our first exercise was her bravery. She is more courageous than some boys her age, and she easily masters the techniques taught [to] her. She has been nicknamed 'Nchout Ajara' by her peers because of her brilliance."

Even though Fleurette's role model is Cameroon's Indomitable Lionesses' goal poacher Nchout Njoya Ajara, the 10-year-old's coach says she is likely to end up as a central defender or a defensive midfielder.

"At her age it is difficult to determine for sure which post she will be most suited for because we let them play all round to detect their strengths.

But looking at her with the eye of a technician and tactician, she has the traits of a defensive midfielder. She can also play as a defender. All we need to do now is coach her into the ideal player we want her to be."

Mbouda, Fleurette's hometown, is one of the towns in Cameroon that hosts games of the country's top tier men's league, the MTN Elite One Championship. The MTN Stadium is the home ground of the Bamboutos FC, finalists in the 2022 Cup of Cameroon and winners of the 2022 FECAFOOT Champions' Cup.

Apart from the regular exercises that Fleurette and her mates are given at the football academy, they assist on match days of the MTN Elite One Championship as ball boys and girls.

"I take Fleurette and her mates to the stadium often because I want them to observe what their seniors in football are doing and learn from them. While picking the balls, they have the opportunity to get first-hand knowledge on the various actions to take on the pitch and how to go about them," said coach Djockeng.

Hurdles to women's football development in Cameroon

Prior to 2020, women's football in Cameroon was limited to the senior women's national team due to poor structuring and lack of media visibility.

Thanks to the brewing company Guinness, women's football has gained increasing public interest through the introduction of the Guinness 'Home Advantage' campaign which included sponsorship of the Cameroon Women's Football League, now known as the Guinness Super League.

However, while the game has increased in popularity, there is still significant room for improvement.

a. Lack of Training Facilities

The Cameroon Football Federation (FECAFOOT) has long had a constitutional responsibility to promote the development of women's and youth football, and to achieve full participation of women in football's governing bodies. However, progress has been slow.

The implementation of strategies to achieve these goals has historically been lackadaisical, with just a few football academies in the country taking interest in coaching young female talent.

The National Football Academy, ANAFOOT was set up in 2014 with branches in all ten regions of Cameroon. It accepts both males and females. For the 2022–2023 season, the west regional branch of ANAFOOT recruited 36 boys and 26 girls. The west regional coordinator, Kamchia Guiffo Guy, attributes the smaller number of female trainees to the reticence of parents to allow their daughters to pursue a career in football. He added that "Generally the number of girls that come knocking on our door every year for the selection test is always three times smaller than that of boys."

To date, only two football academies exist that specialise in identifying and nurturing talents in women's football in Cameroon, and they are both owned by individuals.

Rails Football Academy was set up in 2019 by former Indomitable Lioness striker, Gaëlle Déborah Enganamouit, as the first women's football academy. It only operated for two years. Its activities halted in November 2021 when Enganamouit was accused of being in a same-sex relationship which is illegal in Cameroon, resulting in parents withdrawing their children from the Academy.

The other is the Ngadeu Football Club which has a team that was promoted to the Guinness Super League, Cameroon's top tier women's football league, in 2022–23. It is based in the Adamawa Region of the country with 'Indomitable Lions' captain and 2017 African Cup of Nations (AFCON) winner, Michael Ngadeu-Ngadjui, as an ambassador.

The other twelve professional clubs playing in the Guinness Super League all depend on school and regional competitions to scout for and recruit players.

The West Region where Fleurette lives is yet to have a professional women's football club. Unless the situation changes in the near future, she will be left with no choice but to move away from her family to another part of Cameroon in search of a professional football club—a challenge for any teenager.

b. Unspoken Stigmatisation of Female Footballers

Living in a patriarchal society poses enough challenges for women, but it is even more difficult for female footballers who suffer stigmatisation on a daily basis.

In most communities in Cameroon, it is believed that women should marry, give birth to children and cater to the needs of their families. Some families also believe that some professions are not suitable for women. Football is one of them.

Due to their physiques shaped by the regular physical activity that they do, most female footballers are seen as men and unfit to become wives.

Fleurette might have the support of her immediate family at her tender age but as she matures, the situation could be complex and prejudicial for her. She will need to be tough enough mentally to face the spite of a conservative and patriarchal society as she proceeds on her journey of becoming a professional footballer.

Attacking midfielder for Lekié Filles (one of the Guinness Super League teams), 30-year-old Melvis Ngifor Tantoh, shared her experience: "I have received unfair treatment from my family. They could not bear the fact that I decided to become a footballer. My father even burnt my boots more than three times just to stop me from playing football. But when he realised that I am so passionate about the game, he gave up.

"Society has been treating me like a man. Friends tell me that I dress like a man, I have developed muscles which are not good for a woman and that I will scare men away. My boyfriend told me that he hopes I will not beat him up one day. I told him that no matter what, I remain a woman. It is the love for football that has kept me going because I feel like we are being ostracised by the community."

The media officer for the Under 20 women's national football team, Esther Ayimbo, said: "It is frustrating to see players with low self-esteem caused by the denigrating looks and ill comments from people who tag them as homosexual. But they are gradually changing the narrative. We saw Annette Flore Ngo Ndom with her husband on TV during the Guinness Super League Awards. I think the situation will change for the better in the near future."

Female footballers like former Indomitable Lionesses' shot-stopper Annette Flore Ngo Ndom and defender Claudine Falonne Meffometou Tcheno have proven that women can play football and still maintain a family. Annette is married with two kids while Falonne gave birth a year before representing her country in the 2022 Women's Africa Cup of Nations in Morocco.

c. Poor Remuneration

Before Samuel Eto'o Fils took over as the Cameroon Football Federation president in December 2021, the monthly salaries of footballers plying their trade in the domestic football leagues (i.e. the MTN Elite One and Two Championships and the Guinness Super League) were sporadic and dismal. Players were paid depending on the mood of club presidents. They could go for months without salaries which often led to strike actions that interrupted championships.

In 2021, the basic salaries of players of the women's first division championship (the Guinness Super League) was set at 50,000 CFA francs, approximately USD440. This was to be paid by the official sponsor, Guinness Cameroon. Players in the men's division one championship, the MTN Elite One, received a minimum salary of 100,000 CFA francs (USD890).

Both salary levels were doubled by the Cameroon Football Federation in June 2022 as part of a drive to improve the living conditions of footballers in Cameroon as well as the standards of competition.

Unfortunately, six months later, the Federation reversed their decision on the women's salaries and Guinness Super League players were again earning 50,000 CFA francs. The men's salaries did not revert to their previous level.

The future is bright

Nonetheless, there is hope on the horizon.

Under Samuel Eto'o Fils' leadership, FECAFOOT has signed significant partnership agreements with national and international organisations for the development of both women's and youth football.

The Guinness Super League is now receiving more media attention. Under the previous president of the Cameroon Football Federation, Seïdou Mbombo Njoya, the broadcast rights for the Guinness Super League and the Elite One and Two Championships were acquired by the state broadcaster, Cameroon Radio Television (CRTV).

In December 2022, FECAFOOT and CRTV renewed the collaboration to give more visibility to games of the MTN Elite One and Two Championships, the Cup of Cameroon matches and Guinness Super League games. The increased attention on television and radio has led to greater support for women's football from sports bloggers in the country.

The media visibility of the Guinness Super League has also facilitated the selection of players into the national football teams. One example is Monique Ngock who was picked from Éclair Football Filles de Sa'a to be part of the squad that represented Cameroon at the Women's Africa Cup of Nations in Morocco 2022. Even though Cameroon was eliminated from the competition at the quarter-finals, Monique Ngock's brilliant performance landed her a three-year contract with French Division One side, Stade de Reims.

The Guinness Super League awards are also encouraging healthy competition among women's football players in Cameroon. The awards reward outstanding players such as top goalkeepers, top goal scorers, best coaches, best players, best referees and best clubs of the year.

In May 2022, a partnership agreement between the Cameroon Football Federation and the Cameroon Secondary Education Department was struck to foster national school championships at both secondary school and university levels. The most outstanding students will represent Cameroon in the African Schools Football Championship.

Shortly after the meeting with the Minister for Secondary Education, Professor Pauline Nalova Lyonga, Samuel Eto'o wrote on his social media handles: "Across the country, there are thousands of young boys and girls with a dream to shine on the football pitch and compete with the best. It's an honour to present a newly signed agreement between FECAFOOT and MINESEC. Together, we aim to accelerate the development of youth football in Cameroon, starting with this year's African Schools Championship."

In August 2022, the United Nations Development Programme and the Cameroon Football Federation launched a joint project under the Sport for Development, Peace and Social Cohesion programme. This will result in the construction of 10 multisport complexes across the country, aimed at improving access for women, young people and vulnerable groups to quality sports infrastructure.

Though not directly linked to women's football, the construction of a modern sports complex in the West Region will mean an improvement in the quality of equipment used in training young talents like Fleurette.

Women's football in Cameroon is like a vast unexplored land. There are many opportunities for current and future generations if given the right attention and level of resources.

For Fleurette Lorraine Pelam Zime and her mother Fokou Armande, the future looks much brighter.

Like most supportive mothers, Fokou Armande prays every day that her daughter one day gets to wear the national colours of Cameroon in international competitions at Under 17 and Under 20 levels, and ultimately with the Indomitable Lionesses.

Chansiline Nanze is a broadcast journalist who reports on sports, health, culture and tourism-related issues. A graduate of the Advanced School of Mass Communication (ASMAC Yaoundé), Chansiline bagged the Sports Reporter of the Year award for 2022.

Coconut Football: A Bittersweet Relationship

by Adi Arieta Tinai

Journey through life

It's easy to stand with the crowd. It takes courage to stand alone
—Mahatma Gandhi

I come from an island nation adrift in the middle of the Pacific Ocean. It is a dot on the world map. A country of a mere 900,000 people inhabiting the 300 plus islands that make up our homeland.

'FIJI, THE WAY THE WORLD SHOULD BE' is a cliché I guess—coming from the mouth of a 'horse' who has lived here all her life, trying to grow the sport.

I started playing at the age of eight, straight from school every day, growing up in a house full of girls and a neighbourhood full of boys. My first band-aids were used to cover cuts and bruises from being thrown under the house by boys who would rather use you as a ball girl than accept you as a teammate. After a few years of that, I developed into being the young female, Fiji version of the great Diego Maradona. It was the beginning of my journey to donning a Fiji jersey.

Through high school, my teachers saw me as an asset; I joined the school boys' team and even won the sportswoman of the year award for three consecutive years. Again, this experience helped me develop as a player.

But the journey was tough. I was the first bald-headed girl and tiny (about 5 feet 4 inches, weighing 50 kilograms)—but faster than Speedy Gonzalez—I was the talk of the town.

"Where did she come from?"

"That looks more like a boy?"

"Is that a girl?"

They were some of the many questions I heard whispered through the crowd.

National women's team

Selected for the national team for the first time, I was curious about what it had to offer me, and how much it would mean for them to have me running in the white and black colours.

The Fiji women's football team is named after a unique national bird—the 'kula'—a collared lory (Phigys solitarius), and the team has existed since 1983.

Sadly, our national football website (www.fijifootball.com.fj), with all the history of football clearly stated back to 1938, has everything about men, how their teams started and how successful we have been through the years, but there is nothing about the women's teams.

If you type 'women's football' into the search tab, you will then see all the updates of women's football in the local and Oceania region, but it only states what we are doing now in league games and updates. There is nothing on our official website about our history, our legends, and our best moments as women in football.

It is a sad truth. But by highlighting it, I want to let people know about our silent, ongoing battle for a budget to be set aside for women when it comes to reaching out to the technological world and portraying the world of football for both genders in the media.

It is not until you get into **the system** that you realise you are just a number.

I have seen days that while the Fiji national men's team was accommodated in our $5.5 million National Football Academy—50 women of the same stature had to squeeze into the stadium's change room for accommodation for up to three months at a time to get ready for the Pacific Games. But we loved the Fijian jersey too much to care about our health; we loved the round ball more than money.

Our women also only had an opportunity to see a physiotherapist once a week. I remember breaking the metacarpal bone of my ring finger; I had to sneak out of national camp to seek medical help after staying in my room for three days without a physiotherapist to determine whether I had a broken bone.

While the men had a diet plan, women had to work on an allocated budget. We were told that we could not perform as well as the men, yet in FIFA rankings we were (and still are) a long way ahead.

These were some of the many reasons why representing the 'Noble Banner Blue' was bittersweet. I had great pride in representing my island home. But the bitter part came from our experience compared with the men and, if we dared to speak up, how we were treated.

The battlefield

While playing, I wasted no time in making use of all available resources through people I have met along the way. I started my coaching career while still in the national team, thinking I would make a difference by getting involved more—volunteering, coaching and assisting in any way I could. Having understood where I stand as a coach, I began to raise questions on the qualifications of people who are allowed to take up coaching courses, let alone unqualified coaches who take up posts that are vacant.

Developing football from little to nothing, our governing body banned me for speaking up about equality about a year ago. I have spent more than 20 years in the game, but I fight a battle to be heard.

They stripped me of my coaching licence, they did not allow me to train with my club, and so I do not get a chance to play or be at a football arena at all for media commentary or as a liaison officer with the Samoan team.

As a single mother of two children who is trying to make ends meet, being without a job makes it very tough indeed.

The kula today

Fast-forward to 2023 and after hosting a great tournament (the Oceania Football Confederation Women's Nations Cup in July 2022), we are still trying to comprehend the reasons why women's football in Fiji is still 20 years behind in terms of football culture, development, and most of all equality, in terms of representation at all levels.

According to the latest statistics, there are 19,000 registered football players in Fiji; 17,000 are male and there are only 2,000 females.

Venus Williams once said: "Some people say that I have an attitude—maybe I do. But I think that you have to. You have to believe in yourself when no one else does—that makes you a winner right there."

These exact words were uttered to me when I spoke up about equality.

In 2011, a few big names from Fiji football left for greener pastures—or rather, left to accomplish another milestone in their sporting careers. The move saw 60 percent of women moving to rugby union during football's off season only to be told that they could not return to football in the new season. Players such as Rusila Nagasau (Fiji Rugby 7s captain), Aloesi Nakoci, Litia Naiqato, Elina Taoba, Akisi Taoba, Maryanne Hickes, Lavenia Tinai, Ana Maria Roqica and Vasiti Solikoviti are some of the many individuals that left football.

Not surprisingly, this handful of women went on to be Olympians, securing contracts as far as France and the 'Land of the Rising Sun' (Japan). Football's loss is rugby's gain.

As much as the Oceania Football Confederation (OFC) seeks to build the foundations of women's football in the Pacific in trying to make use of those who aspire to grow or give back to our communities, this statement will never come to pass unless (and until) the OFC demands the empowerment of women in the Fiji Football Association's constitution.

Breaking new ground

Despite the struggle of trying to be heard or seen as an asset to the Fiji Football Association, Everton Sisters Football Club was born through business house competitions in Fiji.

I started registering girls who were seen as not only a threat to Fiji Football but to district teams led by men. Girls who were bullied, girls who were told they were not good enough, girls who could not afford proper training gear, single mothers, school drop-outs and more.

Now the battle begins again. We cannot get qualified referees who sponsors are willing to pay, let alone be recognised for our efforts in growing the sport, or be part of the football fraternity at all. We hosted our first women's competition with four women's teams wearing anything that would make us look like a team.

We borrowed shoes to match the football pitch; we even walked for 32 kilometres just to have a kick in the park. Our first year, we registered 28 ladies. Our second year, we managed to get women in corporate organisations supporting us, where most girls even had their very own water bottles. The first man that believed in our dream was none other than the then Deputy British High Commissioner to Fiji, Mr Paul Welsh, who bought us our first team uniforms and equipment. We began to make it official that Everton Sisters Football Club was our home away from home.

Harrison Ford at 30 was still a carpenter and Vera Wang did not design her first dress until she was 40. I was just starting a ripple at 35.

Today we are Fiji's champions in the women's business house tournament. We have registered more than six women's teams in futsal competitions and have finally been recognised to represent the Suva district. We played our first international futsal match against Australia, losing 4-1.

Everton Sisters FC is the success story of every female footballer in Fiji. Over the past three years, we have sent six young women to join the British Army and they are serving in Wales and Scotland; two are single mothers.

A further four are seasonal workers in Australia now sending money back home to their families. When one door closes, not one opens—hundreds of doors open. I say hundreds due to the fact that I may not type a blog, but I can write an application and make sure that one of my players gets a job. Fiji Football will never secure contracts for A-League Women (Australia's premier women's competition) prospects that we have, yet I accommodate them all in Everton Sisters and make sure they get a secure job with the talent they have.

Someone once said that we concentrate too much on our sorrows and we forget to enjoy the little moments of victory.

My joy is seeing my children enjoy football—despite not being allowed to play with other kids in our football development program since I was banned. My joy is in the children that still meet me in public and have it in them to call me "coach" or "mummy" as I usually give my students the comfort of a parental figure when they need to be heard. My comfort is in the parents who ask to pay me $15 an hour just to train their children in a day. That is trust and respect right there.

In commentary today, I am not only an analyst, I am a coach, I am an entertainer and I am a big part of football.

I have a dream that 20 years from now, my daughter will get to represent the noble banner blue with the pride, joy and freedom that her Constitution allows; that my son will get to play in a team regardless of his sexuality and what he believes in; and that football will be a universal language of freedom and peace.

I cannot wait for the day when Fijian footballers elect half of their board members as women, and actually give them the table upon which to roll their dice.

DEVELOPING WOMEN'S FOOTBALL

Adi Tinai is a single mother who has played for Fiji and she still plays at an elite level in local competition. Her aim is to ensure that the voices of women and girls in football in Fiji are heard and they receive the same conditions and rights as male players and administrators.

For Women Only: Unique Issues for Women in Football

by Neilley Embessa

Menstruation and football competitions do not always mix well. Yet women play football just like their male counterparts—training daily, competing in numerous matches and winning trophies—all while having to deal with the challenges of female biology. Women footballers are subject to their menstrual cycle which can have a significant impact on both their physical and mental state. The impact on a player's performance, which was overlooked for so long by football's governing bodies, is increasingly being recognised and brought to the forefront.

"The menstruation period of female footballers is a subject that is regularly addressed, as mentalities have evolved today compared to some time ago. Menstruation must be addressed and taken into account in women's football to educate and edify the female footballer on her menstrual cycle, the inconveniences caused by it, and try to find solutions to soften or even reduce these unpleasant sensations during menstruation," said Bernadette Anong, assistant coach of the Cameroon national team.

In Cameroon, menstruation is no longer taboo. "It is a subject that is being discussed more. In many training centres, this subject comes up again to prepare the young girl footballer to face the inconveniences caused by the menstrual cycle. The menstrual cycle has an impact on different levels emotionally, physically and in terms of performance. And as the manifestations are different depending on the girl, we talk about it to better prepare them to manage this situation," stated Anong.

In football in particular, menstruation is an inconvenience for players—

whether it be physical or psychological.

Ange Bawou, goalkeeper for the 'Indomitable Lionesses' of Cameroon commented: "My menstrual cycle lasts almost five days and it is usually accompanied by pain in the lower abdomen. It's a time of discomfort and stress because psychologically there are hold-ups during training sessions and certain matches. There are moves you can't make because you're wondering: will my sanitary towel fall off? Will it move? It's little questions like that that you ask yourself when you're in the thick of football training and matches during your period."

It is the same for her national teammate, Melvis Tantoh, whose period limits her performance by affecting her physical condition. "I have severe pain in my lower abdomen for the first two days of my period. This pain, usually coupled with high fatigue, often prevents me from training and being effective on the field—to the point where, in the national team as well as for my club, I have often been asked to do certain sequences or make efforts during my period, and it has been noted that the result is not the same as when I am not bleeding."

According to the national team players, female presence on the coaching staff is helpful and reassuring.

"It's easy to discuss this kind of issue with the ladies and explain the situation. They are always understanding. I was systematically put on rest during the two painful days of my cycle and then I came back as soon as I felt better," explained Tantoh.

Assistant coach Bernadette Anong said players can be impacted in different ways. "Some can feel stronger, some are emotionally affected, weakened or overexcited. Personally, when I was playing, I became a bit more aggressive. As I got older, I developed other symptoms like joint pain and a temporary fever. On the other hand, there are some who can perform well."

Menstruation is also conducive to injury for female footballers as it alters their hormonal levels, and the body is more sensitive to stress during this time. According to one study, the menstrual cycle is an inflammatory process and excessive inflammation can lead to injury.[1]

Indeed, because of the lowered red blood cell and iron levels during menstruation, the menstrual cycle interferes with the performance of high-level players, especially when physical and mental fatigue is noted.

"When a woman is in period, she loses a lot of blood and mineral elements. This can lead to anaemia. I remember a match abroad and one of the national team players had already told me the day before that her period was coming and that it would bother her. She was very upset. I asked her to take iron tablets, drink lots of water and try to relax. The next day, the day of the match, she was in the starting 11, because we said she would be fine. But before the warm-up she called me again to tell me that she was dizzy. I told the head coach and he didn't play her because if we had taken the risk of putting her in, she would certainly get hurt. These are complicated situations that we manage all the time," explained Anong.

The stress of menstruation has led players to demand that clothing manufacturers match their menstrual cycles, particularly in the choice of colours. In July 2022 during the Women's Euro tournament, English and French players asked sponsor Nike to adapt their kit colours to their menstrual cycles.

"It's great to have an all-white outfit, but it's not necessarily suitable when we have our period. We try to deal with it as best we can," England striker Beth Mead told *The Telegraph*.

In October 2022, Puma and Manchester City announced that their women's shorts will no longer be white from the 2023–2024 season, but navy blue. The club explained in a statement that the decision was due to the creation of an environment for female players to "feel comfortable and perform at their highest level. We have always talked about supporting the

---

[1] https://pubmed.ncbi.nlm.nih.gov/22865231/

players as best we can, improving the level of the girls as much as possible, not just at this club, at all levels for women's football."

Understanding the impact of the menstrual cycle on footballers has been helped by the recent increased interest in women's sport in general along with the issue being openly discussed.

"Technical staff must listen to the players," said Bernadette Anong. "In the national team, there are measures taken on the medical level as well as the social level."

Taking account of menstrual cycles could be beneficial for other Cameroonian sports teams too. Starting from the principle that menstruation should not be synonymous with stopping sport, voices are being raised in favour of considering the needs of sportswomen.

"To be able to educate the young female player from her club team and to provide her with means so she is less embarrassed, these are points on which we must improve to have a better performance. Similarly, we need to treat and value players who are mothers better, such as regularising their salary situation."

Anong says she is pleased that the Guinness Super League and the Cameroon Football Federation (FECAFOOT) kept their commitments regarding the salaries of players in 2022.

"Today, women footballers feel a little more autonomous and can manage themselves, which is something to be encouraged, but we still have a long way to go," she concluded.

Football and motherhood

Another juggle for some women players is motherhood. Just like menstruation, pregnancy and childbirth are subjects that are often put aside.

At present, FIFA requires its member associations to provide a minimum period of 14 weeks of paid maternity leave for professional players at a minimum of two-thirds of their salaries. At least 8 of those weeks must be taken immediately after the birth of the child.

Coach Anong believes that at the national level "women footballers who are mothers must be treated and valued so that they are not left out of the picture or marginalised. Their salaries should be paid regularly so that they can take care of their children. Stable funding enables them to give their best."

It requires a lot of focus, time and attention to be a mother, and without a supportive partner, it can be difficult for players who are mothers to continue at the same level as a player.

On the other hand, there are some who are able to manage their lives as footballers and mothers with ease. They manage to concentrate on trying to do their best as mothers and as professional footballers. Coaches pay special attention to this, especially in the case of major competitions.

Coach Bernadette Anong: "We give consideration to mother players on two levels. When their children are still small, during training sessions the child's partner can bring the child all the time so that the mother can see the child and she can feed him /[her]. In 2016, during the African Cup of Nations for women held in Cameroon, we had this case with the national goalkeeper Annette Ngo Ndom who had just given birth four months earlier. We wrote to the Minister of Sports at the time, Mr. Pierre Ismaël Bidoung Kpwatt, to ask him to authorise the child and his father to come to the Indomitable Lionesses' training camp so that he could be easily fed. This was done.

"For the player whose child is no longer small, we allow the child to be brought [to camp] from time to time so that his mother is less tense and can concentrate better and performs better."

Anong said that players who are mothers tend to display the same traits in training camp.

"I have coached mother footballers. They are a little more attentive than the other players. They are the most protective of the group and they have a particular contribution to make in educating the other girls and in discipline. They make an effort to be exemplary both on and off the field. Maybe it's because they have children. If they have a problem with their offspring, they tell the coach. This makes them feel more comfortable and freer, knowing that at any moment they can be called upon to deal with the case of this child. They don't find it difficult to express themselves and look after the other players in the group. "

Watford and Wales striker Helen Ward told FIFPRO (the Fédération Internationale des Associations de Footballeurs Professionnels) in an interview in 2021 about her own experiences of balancing motherhood and a playing career: "It's very important for young girls to realise that having a family doesn't mean stopping living. I always thought that having children would be the end of my football career, but when I got pregnant with my daughter over seven years ago, I just wasn't ready to stop my career. There were starting to be more and more cases of women footballers continuing to play as mothers, such as England player Katie Chapman, and they were real role models, showing the way to have children and return to the top level.

"In fact, being a mother has enhanced my career and strengthened me as a person. Before I had a child, I could mope about a bad match result for five days after a match, whereas now I just don't have time to mope about it. I come home and my kids ask me for a hug or a treat and suddenly the bad result is not the end of the world.

"That's not to say that results don't matter to me as much as they used to, but I've developed a better sense of priorities. This new ability to compartmentalise my life between football and family has worked really well for me in my career."

As a strategy to encourage the growth and development of the women's game, it is vital that policies are implemented and action taken to improve the awareness of the impact of the menstrual cycle, pregnancy, and childbirth on women players at all levels.

Neilley Ebessa is editor-in-chief of Kick442.com, an online news website dedicated to football in Cameroon. She is a graduate of the Ecole Supérieure de Communication de Mass (ASMAC) with a special interest in Cameroonian women's football.

The Shine of Women and Girls in Brazilian Soccer: An Illustrated Story

by Nathalia Servadio

Mary Wollstonecraft wrote in her 1792 book, *A Vindication of the Rights of Women* (2017, p. 69), that: "It is time to give them [women] back their lost dignity—and make them part of the human species."

When we think about the dignity and right of different girls and women to play sports (including football), this claim is just as relevant today. Giving them back their dignity means highlighting their brilliance and allowing their freedom of expression.

In Brazilian football, the shine of women is overshadowed. The sports opportunities for them are unequal and mainly marked by symbolic and political impediments. For example, the political impediments to the practice of sport by women between 1941 and 1979,[2] further delegitimised them.

The shine of women may have been overshadowed—but it has never been erased. They have continued to fight for their sporting space, creating their own strategies to take advantage of a space that is rightfully theirs: "And today, in the 21st century, girls play everywhere, they play very well, and they even play in the Olympics. All because a handful of girls decided to fight for their rights."[3]

Inspired to share this glittering glow of Brazilian women's football, I'm going to tell you a little bit of the story of a community of players who fought to keep shining in football and also in futsal. They teach us that the struggle, when done collectively, becomes more potent—the glow can turn into a flame to light up more people, shining brighter and further!

Initial kick-off

During my master's degree in education and social sciences at the State University of Campinas,[4] I was concerned with investigating the development of girls and women in Brazilian football—identifying actions and opportunities that would allow them to shine like stars.

---

[2] The National Sports Council (CND) prohibited by law the practice of sports considered inappropriate for girls and women.

[3] Excerpt from the book "Leila Menina" written by Ruth Rocha, Brazilian writer of children's literature.

[4] Public university located in the interior state of São Paulo, Brazil.

As a researcher and player, I saw this endeavour as a political struggle. We found that different girls and women abandon playing football in Brazil and/or are often not encouraged to participate. We sought to discover spaces/projects that offered football practice for girls and women.

I found, participated in and investigated a project that has been offering soccer and futsal exclusively for women of different generations for more than two decades—something rarely found in the national territory. We interviewed hundreds of participants from different generations in this project, including fans, family members, players and professionals. They shared their experiences within a project aimed exclusively at girls and women playing soccer.

The project studied was the Projeto Futebol Feminino Campinas. It is run in Campinas, 68 kilometres north-west of the city of São Paulo in partnership with a social club. Its formation was the result of a long trajectory of battles, and it offers hundreds of girls and women a space to experience football and shine together.

The social club that initially partnered with the project had previously only designated a spectator role for female members. However, there were women who were not satisfied with this role and who struggled daily for change.

The women's demands to play football began with the action of some local mother-members in 1996, and, later, this was transformed into the Campinas Women's Football Project. They were responsible for legitimising the beginning of female football, seven-a-side and futsal within the association. They paved the way for more girls, women and trans-men from the Campinas region to shine and they expanded their membership boundaries beyond the upper–middle social strata.

As we will see in this story, girls and women have subverted social stigmas and manoeuvres to claim (and remain in) this football space. The Campinas Women's Football Project was responsible for kick-starting the female game and creating a football team in the late 1990s.

Warming up: creating a team of women

Sueli[5] was one of the women who did not allow herself to be just a spectator and supporter. She preferred to act as a protagonist in the transformation of the social club. She related that in the halls of the club in the 1990s, she loved "playing ball" with her three-year-old son. Sports spaces are responsible for both the construction and deconstruction of gender inequalities. As the women sought to occupy these spaces in the social club, they faced strategies and natural barriers from the community and their family members:

"When my youngest saw me enter the field to hit a ball during the break of his father's game, he saw me and said, 'No Mum, yes Dad,' so imagine what was going on in his head? That made a big impression on me," Sueli said sadly.

Sueli felt a "very strong adrenaline rush" when wanting to join in and play the game at the club. According to her, this passion came from her childhood when she played with her brothers. However, outside her home, she was impeded and discouraged from playing:

"It was a passion, [but] I only played in the garage with my brothers and it was a healthy game there," commented Sueli, but when it went outside, it was a game that "hurt".

Outside of a safe space to play football, many girls and women experienced different forms of violence: "It was scary for anyone outside to see me with a three-year-old son and play soccer," admitted Sueli.

Girls and women were under constant surveillance by the community to fit into gender norms, especially when indicating their interest in soccer lessons: "They would say to me with a surprised face: 'So you, with children, why are you playing?'" Sueli recalled.

---

[5] Names used are fictitious to preserve the identity of participants. Sueli participated in the Project for 5 years.

Vilma was another woman who was inspired to join the cause and she commented on the process of creating a female team at the club: "There was a team of boys—why can't we too? Let's put together a women's team. That's when we knocked on the director's door!"

Subsequently, the board of the social club announced the "possible" opening of a women's football class in the club's activities but they would not guarantee it.

Sueli raced to sign up. However, she discovered that before the female class would be "validated" as a club activity, the enrolment of at least 10 girls/women was necessary so the class could be run separately from the boys/men.

However, the initial participation by the female members was inconsistent, making it difficult to keep the group class activity in the social club's schedule. Sueli recalled that she and her colleagues invited fellow members to participate and achieve stable numbers in the fight for a permanent space in the club's activity timetable: "I invited the other mothers and they didn't go. They didn't go for everything from prejudice to fear. They said they did not agree with an aggressive practice," said Sue.

The associates who were afraid of football at the time were mostly white and middle or upper-class young people who were expected to marry and have a child "early". Many of these women who frequented the club were self-employed (and called "housewives" by Sueli). They found it strange that football was even played by women. This fear was associated with the long-held concept of social roles within the country.

Entering the field: The shine of player mothers

Sueli recalled that at the time [1993], she had no experience with other contact and strength sports, and the birth of her son also imposed new limitations: "I got married very early and some people there [at the club] didn't like to see a mother playing."

The association between being a mother and a player was non-existent for the local community: "The mothers got scared, they said in surprise: 'Do you play football?' It was like that. 'Wow, you?' As if it was strange, I took it personally," Sueli explained.

This questioning—raising doubts about the viability of being a mother and a player—can be seen as a daily stigma faced by those women.

The conformity of women to their reproductive role and their ability to bear healthy children has long been part of Brazilian history. Football is one of the sports that both governments and Brazilian medical practitioners sought to "distance" from women from as far back as the 19th century on the grounds that it would bring risks on their path to motherhood. The player-mother notion went against the grain of social imagination.

When playing soccer, the player-mothers resisted these gender norms. They blurred the notion of femininity and motherhood as their innate destiny.

"I remember well when I started playing, I was about 23 years old and I already had a three-year-old son at the time; it was a joy to start playing and that was what motivated me to continue, because I got married very early and since high school I haven't had the opportunity to learn more about and practise women's football," reported Vilma.

Over the years, football practice became a space for learning and belonging to women like Vilma: "A lot of what I lived through in football formed who I am today—understanding the pain of the other. Sport made me work as a team and see that as a team/collective we can go far. Belonging to the team makes the difference. We lean on each other, that makes us grow," she confessed.

The energy of being player-mothers, despite facing social challenges, provided them with a sense of belonging in the sport. It's a feeling they want to pass on to their children: "When I had the second child I eventually wanted to go back. Then it was cool, the mother playing on the line, the youngest on the wing and the eldest on the goal!" laughed Sueli.

First goals

Sueli, Vilma and so many other player-mothers began to inspire more and more people to practise with them. Numbers have increased by leaps and bounds over the years. They have been supported by some more progressive sports policies that have emerged in the country such as the Sports Incentive Law[6] and the Sports Investment Fund in Campinas (FIEC).[7] Now, not not

---

[6] http://rededoesporte.gov.br/en/incentives/lei-de-incentivo-ao-esporte

[7] https://portal.campinas.sp.gov.br/noticia/3015

only club members can take classes, but non-members from different locations, races and classes in the city of Campinas and the surrounding region. They have experienced football with other women for the first time, participating in training and championships in the region. Along with the first team of mothers, they have formed the basis of the Campinas Women's Football Project.

The insertion of non-member players in the club makes the environment more diverse, with women not only of different age groups, but of various social and cultural origins, sexual orientations, income, etc.

"[A] diversity of women from all over the city, of all bodies, colours, cultures and social classes ride on buses to get there," exclaimed Katia.[8]

The interest of children and young female soccer players from Campinas was huge and with limited or non-existent options elsewhere in the city, the soccer spaces of the social club were increasingly being occupied by females. The arrival of more players from different parts of the city opened the doors of a space traditionally reserved for the middle and upper class. The growth forced the club to hold classes grouped by age: up to 12 years, 13 to 15 years, 16 to 18 years and over 18 years. The visibility of teams also started to increase in the city and, after four years, the number of girls participating in the project reached around 60.

They were building a connection beyond just the practice of sports.

"We are many, different, but at the same time we are a whole... a whole in favour of women's football," exclaimed Leticia.[9]

"Here we are a family, no matter how difficult things may be, we have each other," Zagueira Leticia chimed in.

Exchanges that have been socially developed over the years of practice at the club offer feelings of connection in terms of the political struggle for

---

[8] A non-social player

[9] A player who spent more than 10 years in the project.

women. They have fostered a sense of belonging in the community. The feeling of belonging in football that was denied to them for a long time has been expressed in multiple ways. Many girls have benefitted from the free food, psychological counselling and English classes offered at the club to nurture their potential to develop a possible sports career or studies in the area.

Red card: player evasions and the overshadowed shine

A change of directors at the social club and the higher number of players ultimately led to the charging of monthly fees—access to the club was restricted to those who were able to pay.

"The club came and said...'Look, the girls here can't train anymore! Because they have to pay the monthly fee, because we have to pay you'" commented Mauro[10] angrily.

The return to charging monthly fees was a response to the movement of members, mostly from the upper-middle class. They started to leave the

---

[10] Mauro has worked in the Campinas Women's Football Project as a coach since the creation of the first team and currently coordinates the entire Project.

recreational clubs in Campinas for the growing condominiums in the urban areas of the city (which had private spaces for supposedly more interesting leisure activities). Furthermore, the popularisation of gyms and personal trainer services, promising a more individualised and comfortable practice of physical activity, was also mentioned by the interviewees.

Only approximately 15% of the club's female players were able to pay the amount requested to continue training. Players who were unable to contribute were dismissed: "There were 50, 60 girls I had, [then] there were only 5 left, because only 5 or 6, I think maximum 10, paid monthly fees at that time… The others did not. What happened was the girls were just sent away," commented Mauro.

Game break

In the sieve of who stays and who leaves based on their economic and social condition, the project scenario drastically changed. However, this story does not end here. The Campinas Women's Football Project has been kept alive over the past 10 years even in the midst of so many exclusions.

During the writing of this story, a tragedy occurred: the brightness of one of the members of this project, and my friend, was erased on Earth with her passing. I believe her brightness was erased here to become a true star in the sky—to light the way for many children and young people here.

In memory of Carol, I invite you to remember that the flame that crosses all of us can also illuminate you. Just as it moved the mother-players who shared their flame with more women to shine together in football. They also show us that their glow has not dimmed amid so many challenges. It continues radiating on the field.

The Campinas Women's Football Project is important in the Brazilian context of barriers and difficulties in establishing dignity for women in sports. Unfortunately, I didn't have the opportunity to experience playing football in my childhood. As a child, I was prevented and discouraged from playing—but today, I am not only playing but also teaching and training future participants in this sport. It's never too late to radiate your flame!

Nathalia Servadio has a masters in education and social sciences and an undergraduate degree in sports sciences. She is currently working in children's coaching programs with the Brazilian Football Confederation.

Changing the Game

How Viktoria Berlin is Revolutionising Women's Football in Germany

by Alina Ruprecht

On a crisp but sunny Sunday in November, plenty of supporters are gathered at Stadium Lichterfelde, which is located in a south-western suburb of Berlin. It's Matchday 10 in the German Women's Regional League and the game between FC Viktoria Berlin and Türkiyemspor is underway. The atmosphere at the so-called 'Berlin Derby' is relaxed, but expectant.

Many supporters of Viktoria Berlin are sporting the club's colour, sky blue, and wearing sweatshirts from its merchandising range. The words "Game Changer" are printed on the shirts and the fans wear them with visible pride.

A historical derby

A diverse range of people can be found in the crowd, including young girls with their parents, who dream of becoming professional football players. Their eyes light up when the players—their idols—step onto the pitch. University students and groups of women mingle with groundhoppers. Many are laughing and holding a beer can in their hands. Everyone is welcome at Stadium Lichterfelde, whether they are a hardcore football fan or a newcomer to the women's game.

Loud cheers and clapping from the fans echo around the ground as the ball hits the back of the net. Marlies Sänger of Viktoria Berlin has just extended her team's lead. The midfielder's goal sealed the side's 2–1 win over their biggest rivals in the Regional League—the three points gained are vital in the hard-fought battle for the championship title and promotion to the Second Frauen-Bundesliga.

This edition of the Berlin Derby was one for the history books. For the first time, a game from the Women's Regional League was broadcast live on German public television. "It's not just another milestone for Viktoria, but for women's football in general," said Lisa Währer, one of the co-founders of the team, in an interview with Sport1: "Visibility creates change," she emphasised. Nearly 180,000 viewers followed the game in front of their screens, making these words become even more meaningful.

Nothing less...

While Viktoria Berlin is a traditional club with a long history in German football, their women's team is perceived as a new 'lighthouse' project. Since July 2022, has been led by six female "founders", as they call themselves, and run as an outsourced, private and limited company. These six are no strangers to those who follow German women's football closely. Among them are former German international, world and European champion Ariane Hingst, journalist Felicia Mutterer and business expert Verena Pausder. The group of six is completed by Lisa Währer, Katharina Kurz and Tanja Wielgoss.

All of them have a professional background in sports or business. This enables them to combine their various skills with their broad networks for Viktoria Berlin's women's team. "That's exactly what's exciting about our group, this diversity, coming from all areas, really covering a lot of professional ground and thus already having a broad base as a start-up network," explained Ariane Hingst when speaking to Deutschlandfunk. The founders had been unhappy with the development of the women's game in Germany for a while, and they decided to take action.

...But a revolution

This female-led football team and their start-up-inspired business model are an absolute novelty in the country. Just over three-quarters of the company belongs to the founders, 23.9 percent of shares are held by investors, while the Viktoria Berlin club owns the other one percent. "I know that in football, in particular, we have such outdated, dusty structures that finally have to be broken up," said Ariane Hingst. "And I think it's a huge thing for us to say that we have six women in this position, including managing directors, who are taking over the whole thing to drive it forward."

Most of the investors are professionals and well-known people from different sectors of German public life, such as journalist Dunja Hayali, comedian Carolin Kebekus and former pro-athlete Franziska van Almsick. They all contributed single donations ranging between four- and five-digit amounts. Other celebrities act as ambassadors for the club.

The team behind Viktoria Berlin firmly believe in their idea and view it as a revolutionary one. Their overall aim is to "change the German sports world in the long term", as stated in an official press release. "The project is also a kind of a women's movement to make women more visible in sport and give them more of the spotlight," said Lisa Währer in an interview with Deutsche Welle. "Because that has really been very neglected."

American inspiration

Currently, no football team from Berlin plays in the Frauen-Bundesliga. Turbine Potsdam and VfL Wolfsburg are the only clubs from the German women's top-flight competition that are reasonably close to the capital. However, things look different in the men's Bundesliga, where Union Berlin and Hertha BSC both proudly represent the city. The latter recently terminated their financial support for Turbine Potsdam, who were in a tough battle to avoid relegation, to invest in the foundation of their own women's team. Meanwhile, Union Berlin has a squad competing in the same league as Viktoria Berlin.

The group of six founders, the majority of whom grew up in the German capital, didn't want to accept the situation of having no football team from

Berlin in the Frauen-Bundesliga. "For me personally as a Berliner, to be able to develop women's football in my home town and to ensure that we hopefully have a Bundesliga club in a few years' time is of course a matter close to my heart," explained Ariane Hingst. "We certainly have different motivations. In any case, all six founders are enthusiastic about football, [and] also interested in women's football."

In 2020, they found inspiration when Angel City FC was established on the American West coast. Like Berlin, Los Angeles wasn't represented in top-flight women's football in the US, the National Women's Soccer League (NWSL). Actress Natalie Portman initiated the foundation of the new club that started playing in 2022. Plenty of other prominent women, among them Serena Williams and Jennifer Garner, support the project as investors and co-owners. It is a football team "by women for women" with the aim to tackle gender-based inequality both on and off the pitch.

"We liked this idea a lot, to build something based on a network," Katharina Kurz said in an interview with rbb24. She, Felicia Mutterer and a friend discussed the initial idea about kicking off a project like Angel City FC in Germany. This was the starting point of their project for a women's team at Viktoria Berlin.

Two types of goals

The aims of Viktoria Berlin are based on three pillars: football, community and culture. Sporting and socio-political aims go hand in hand. However, the founders face a risky balance, as the team's success on the pitch hugely influences the achievement of their goals outside the sporting area. If the performances and results aren't convincing, it would become difficult to recruit new investors and ambassadors. Generally, the female-led team pushes for changes on all levels wherever they believe it is necessary. As women's football is continuously developing, the goals of Viktoria Berlin tend to be complex and ambitious.

Apart from promotion to the Frauen-Bundesliga in 2025, the club aims to make women in sport more visible and to strive for more equality in women's football. The culture at the club is marked by the belief in beneficial social changes throughout society, sports and football. A statement from the website of Viktoria Berlin emphasises this: "We stand for diversity and inclusion, sustainability, and self-confidence. We want to create a sports and social setting that actively lives and communicates equal opportunities and equal rights. Our goal is to make even more role models from sport visible and to inspire young girls and women." Throughout the strong community at Viktoria Berlin, people with different backgrounds should be brought together. In addition, those who aren't already enthusiastic about women's football should be motivated by the club's diverse network to become supporters.

The founders believe that women's football is economically attractive and they want to create a solid foundation and structures that are sustainable over the long term in order to create both sporting and economic success. Another statement on the club's website highlights that: "We act entrepreneurially and rely on a strong and unique network of politics, business, culture/media, and sport. We not only strive for football success, but also stand for a sustainable and social female movement and want to contribute to social debates."

As most women's teams are part of a club that has primarily been established for the men's game and adapted to its structures, the founders of Viktoria Berlin's women's team want to introduce a differentiated marketing strategy.

By developing their team into a brand of its own, new ways of storytelling are made possible. This is beneficial for the game. "The most important thing is, and one can certainly say as a core statement: We want to create a Viktoria Berlin women's football brand and go a little different way," said Ariane Hingst.

The top is the aim

The six founders knew that they couldn't just 'copy and paste' the concept of Angel City and apply it to a different system. While the American team could just buy a license to play in their highest domestic league, this is not possible in Germany. Viktoria Berlin must play their way into the Frauen-Bundesliga. The promotion to the women's top-flight competition before 2025 is the team's biggest sporting goal. If they continue their successful run, the chances of reaching this goal are high. At the time of writing (early May 2023), Viktoria Berlin sat in first place in the Regional League with an impressive goal difference of 119.

How come these six women didn't found a new club, but took over an existing one instead? "If we had really started a completely new one, we would have had to begin in the District League," explained Katharina Kurz. Therefore, they looked for a club where the first women's team was already playing in a higher tier so that they could "spin them off, take them over and manage them independently".

Other famous football clubs from Germany have introduced their newly established women's teams in a different way. For example, Borussia Dortmund Women were founded in 2021 and started in the lowest league. One year later, they were promoted to the next tier. Those responsible at the club call it, "the Dortmund way", but have formulated the clear aim for the team to reach the Frauen-Bundesliga as soon as possible. However, the earliest point in time this could happen is the 2027/28 season.

From idea to reality

The six female founders at Viktoria Berlin didn't want to wait as long as teams like Borussia Dortmund Women to reach the top German competition. In 2021, they presented their project idea to several Berlin-based clubs—Viktoria Berlin was the one that showed sincere interest.

The founders encountered "people with open ears and willingness, who were enthusiastic about the idea," Ariane Hingst recalled. Verena Pausder shared similar impressions in an interview with *Emotions Magazine*: "At FC Viktoria, the doors were open from the start and there was a great willingness to risk this experiment with us."

With the outsourcing of the women's team as a private limited company, a highly important step was taken before the project started to unfold. Women's football and the women's team had always had a high priority at Viktoria Berlin. However, the persons responsible had never previously found a way to make something more from the good foundation that was already in place at the club. Now, "the topic of women's football will be upgraded in terms of content, will be appreciated more and can act accordingly as a separate company," FC Viktoria's managing director Peer Jaekel explained when speaking to rbb24 in 2022. "The last few weeks and months have shown how women's football is on the rise. (…) Of course, this feeds such a vision."

Jaekel was referring to some record attendances in 2022. Two German clubs, VfL Wolfsburg and FC Bayern Munich, competed in the UEFA Women's Champions League. In the semi-finals, the She-wolves came up against women's football force, FC Barcelona. The first leg was played at the legendary Camp Nou and saw the setting of a new record for a women's football game in Europe—91,648 spectators. For the second leg at the Volkswagen Arena in Wolfsburg, more than 20,000 tickets were sold. Then for the first time in their history, the women's team from FC Bayern Munich played a game at the Allianz Arena. They met Paris St. Germain in a quarter-final clash in front of 13,000 fans. Other Champions League games without the involvement of German teams reached similar attendance numbers.

The new hype

All European women's competition matches are now streamed live and free on DAZN. This provides immediate visibility for the women's game. The new hype about women's football was also fuelled by the UEFA Women's Euros 2022. The attendance of 87,192 fans at the final at Wembley Stadium between Germany and England proved that the momentum of the sport wasn't just a short-term phenomenon—it was the start of a new era.

At the beginning of the 2022/23 season, nearly 700 supporters attended Viktoria Berlin's opening home game against Union Berlin. This was an unusually high number for the women's Regional League. Even some Frauen-Bundesliga teams struggle to sell that many tickets. It shows that the new hype around the women's game has reached new dimensions, and it still has enormous potential to grow. In the context of Germany, this interest can be traced back to the German women's football national team reaching the final of the 2022 UEFA Women's Euros. Despite their narrow defeat in that game against England, the German national team's campaign put the country back on the football map. It generated visibility and demand like never before for the women's game. After the tournament, one attendance record chased the other in the Frauen-Bundesliga. 2022 showed what is possible for women's football around the world, and there is more to come.

Viktoria Berlin recognised the highly increased public interest in women's football and wanted to contribute to it. "But it was also clear to us that someone had to come from outside to provide even more targeted support for women's and girls' football, economically as well as with an expertise in where and how to acquire players and coaches," explained Viktoria Berlin's sporting director, Rocco Teichmann in an interview with rbb24. He described the founders as "shareholders, who are really interested in giving women's football a little more value, but at the same time letting Viktoria Berlin participate in it".

Equal play before equal pay

The founders have continuously emphasised that the 'value' of women's football doesn't have to reach the financial dimensions of the men's game. Instead, they push for "equal play before equal pay". This is about creating professional infrastructures and environments to enable women's football teams to thrive. Ariane Hingst pointed out that investments in women's football are necessary to "give the players the opportunity to play at the highest level and to be a real pro-athlete".

Both the Regional League and the Frauen-Bundesliga aren't fully professionalised tiers. Those clubs who can (and want) to support their women's teams provide well-educated and full-time staff. Other resources can include training pitches and facilities that the players don't have to share with anyone else. Viktoria Berlin is not able to tick off all these boxes yet, but they aim to have fully professionalised structures within the club by the time they secure promotion to the first tier. Now, the players train approximately four times a week. Most of them work a second job as they can't make a living just from football. This is also the case for many players in the Frauen-Bundesliga.

Viktoria Berlin aims to tackle this issue and is leading by example. Many players in the women's Regional League don't earn any money from playing football—Viktoria Berlin is the exception. The club currently pays its players a small salary and provides them with health insurance. "It's healthier to grow slowly than to go from 0 to 1000," Ariane Hingst admitted in another interview with Sport1. "Full professionals in the Regional League, that would be desirable, but we don't even have that all across the Frauen-Bundesliga. It is important to rethink: fair pay is absolutely necessary, but also equal play. In other words, structural requirements that are comparable to men. It's not about millions of salaries for women, no. It's about fair pay and better conditions."

The thrilling campaign of the German women's national team at the 2022 Euros sparked a public debate in Germany over whether the players should be paid the same salaries as their male counterparts. Many other sporting nations, such as the United States and Nordic countries, have already implemented equal pay at the national team level. However, the public debate in Germany has since died down. Projects like the one at Viktoria Berlin have the power and potential to restart such important discussions and unite those fighting for changes and making a difference, even if it is just a small one.

What's next?

Viktoria Berlin's women's team needs to deliver good sporting performances to promote the club and gain more investors. If the team continues to bag three points against difficult opponents like Türkiyemspor, they will be able to celebrate promotion to a higher league. Ariane Hingst is optimistic about the sporting future of Viktoria Berlin: "We are on a very, very good path. I think the way the team plays is attractive and engaging. Sure, the bottom line is that the three points count, but it's all the nicer when that happens with a good offensive game."

Whether football and start-up-inspired business are a good fit remains to be seen. At this point in time, the founders can't make any financial promises to investors. Those who put money into the women's team at Viktoria Berlin cannot know if they will be paid back the same or a higher amount. For everyone involved, it is a financial risk. However, it seems to be a risk worth taking. Women's football has the potential to grow strongly, especially in Germany where a new TV deal will provide even more visibility for the domestic game from the 2023/24 season onwards.

Alina Ruprecht is from Munich and is currently studying for a masters in European studies, while also working in PR and Communications for DAZN. She is an active fan and blogger who covers German women's football for fan site www.90min.de.

Boardroom to Bleachers: Representation and Societal Issues in Football

by Rebecca Ngoie

As the modern game evolves, footballers are confronted with the challenge of being authentic, vulnerable and transparent within the confines of expected public perception.

For all the decorated history, symbolism and passion that it incorporates, football is ultimately in the entertainment industry. It is made relevant and widely publicised by groups of individuals united by their enthusiasm and common interest. It extends an invitation that transcends the societal barriers of age, gender, race and religion, making it a welcome spectacle to be enjoyed by anyone and everyone who appreciates what is fondly regarded as "the beautiful game".

I like to imagine a footballer's career as a blank canvas upon which life paints a unique and customised picture of its own choosing. Not the carefully and intricately curated portraits however; more of the abstract, uncoordinated and seemingly haphazard style—the paintings that appear as if the artist had merely dipped their brush in several colours of paint and excitedly whipped it across the canvas several times over until a work of art emerged. The beauty lies not only in the eye of the beholder. It is also open to infinite interpretation through the lens of those who may set their gaze upon it.

As illustrious and complex as the beautiful game may be, those who bear the honour and responsibility to play the sport are often perceived in a linear manner. As much as a footballer's primary objective is to entertain from the spectators' point of view, the high demands, entitlement and expectations that accompany this duty may paint over the human aspects that footballers possess, in addition to contributing to the pressurised climate in which they attempt to build their livelihoods.

When the intrinsic yearning within any individual to be understood, seen and accepted is met by the volatile, demanding and subliminally dictating nature of fandom and the media, we see several themes emerge which span the broader spectrum of discrimination, representation and mental health issues. There are also ruinous habits and decisions that may be consequences of these silent 'wrestles'.

Professionalism in any workplace is one of the fundamental pillars that help to ensure an environment that thrives upon a code of conduct and cohesion between colleagues. By laying down a marker of expected etiquette, industries set a precedent for how employees ought to present themselves in order to be favourably perceived.

Yet in a game which thrives on characters and personalities as much as it does on the technical aspect of the sport itself, the freedom of a footballer's expression appears to be threatened by the expectation to strictly adhere to a certain mould. The challenge for footballers lies in establishing a healthy equilibrium between adhering to the expected etiquette, while still allowing for their freedom of expression in the game.

Freedom of expression in modern football is no set phenomena. It can be manifested in several different ways. From exhilarating and awe-inducing skills to celebrations of dance and tributes; or from raising awareness on a social issue to advocating for various other campaigns, footballers can offer fans a glimpse into the essence of themselves as honest and authentic individuals to become unique and relatable.

The irony, however, lies in the fact that in an age where freedom of expression should be a free gift to all individuals, footballers find themselves stifled by expectations, condemned by criticisms, and contending with public conflicts and burdens.

The modern game has a host of social issues that contribute to the challenges that footballers face today. There are the obvious and glaring ones in the form of racism, sexual orientation, representation and discrimination toward women and people with a disability in the game. There are also what may be considered underrated strongholds such as shame, guilt, the weight of expectations and abhorrent abuse—these are silent killers that many individuals harbour. These issues can fester and further compound matters when left unaddressed. The ability of all these factors to either derail or stagnate a player's career should not to be disregarded.

Representation

Through its incredible reach, football possesses the unique ability to inspire positive change and to steward social impact initiatives. From presidents and club officials in boardrooms to the everyday fan in stadium bleachers, the responsibility to curate a societal climate in which footballers of all races, genders, ethnic groups, religions and nationalities are able to co-exist without bias and discrimination ought to be a consistently unified effort from top to bottom.

While even the greatest legends in the game have suffered racist abuse and discrimination (like Diego Maradona during his time as a footballer for Italian club Napoli), we need not cast our minds back so far for yet another example of the uphill battle that we face against racial injustice and abuse.

July 11, 2021, marked a momentous milestone in English football history with the men's national team having reached a major tournament final for the first time since 1966. Unfortunately for the UEFA Euro host nation, the final result did not favour the 'Three Lions'. They fell to Italy following a penalty shootout that saw Marcus Rashford, Jadon Sancho and Bukayo Saka all fail to convert their opportunities.

The immediate, vile and abhorrent onslaught of abuse that inundated their social media platforms was unbecoming of a society that ought to be better educated and conducted. It revealed an alarming proportion of society who are non-receptive to a team that welcomes diverse individuals.

It was the moment that the penny dropped. Members of the football community who identify as people of colour acknowledged that the fight for equality and respect was far from over. It was a heartbreaking time; a challenging time. It invoked feelings of uproar, anger and anguish. We can read about stories like these every day and perhaps grow indifferent to them, but the weight and impact of it all is felt way more when it's closer to home.

The response toward footballers of marginalised groups speaks to the nature of their experience and feeds into the way in which they conduct themselves and approach their public image. It instils a 'tip-toe tactic' in which they become incredibly conscious of how the things they do—both on and off the field—may act as a trigger for yet more abuse or criticism. Any mistake, misunderstood quote, footballing error or perceived character flaw becomes a stick used to beat them with.

Mad to missionary

The challenge of advocating for representation across the board begins with us—the under-represented and misunderstood groups ourselves. And it may seem unfair—having to take on the responsibility and bear the weight of a situation that has been thrust upon you—yet it simultaneously places a degree of control back within our grasp.

It's a degree of control that may just be the catalyst for a new lease of life. One in which the adversity of days gone by has been utilised for the betterment of ourselves, our communities and a society that is reflective of a world we want to see.

Righteous anger is the fuelling agent that inspires change. It is more concerned with condemning the misdeed and the injustice, as opposed to the individuals who exhibit and enforce these behaviours. Rightful anger and indignation—when channelled toward efforts of change—can be used as a tool for transformation. It is an anger that should be redemptive in nature without being a stumbling block for those who are open to learning. It is justified and unapologetic in its outrage, discomfort and displeasure while extending a welcome and receptive gesture that offers education and connection.

The unfortunate reality is that many individuals who possess an ignorant or prejudicial outlook on social issues within football do so as a result of a learnt bias or prejudice. People can only be held accountable when they hold an awareness, which places the emphasis once more on education.

As standard bearers and willing activists for change in the modern game, we bear the responsibility to encourage and host more conversations, to create more spaces for people to be brave and more opportunities for people to learn, and more importantly to unlearn their preconceived ideas.

It may not always be the case that people are unaware of an issue—perhaps that issue has just been grossly misrepresented to them. While wilful ignorance and defiant denial in the face of new knowledge ought to be condemned; situational ignorance due to upbringing and exposure serves as an opportunity to rewrite false narratives. The aim is not to silence, but to encourage people to listen and change their ways of thinking. It requires the ill-informed to maintain a posture of being teachable and honest, recognising that it is possible to change biases—even if they were unaware that they ever held them. An individual is less likely to maintain a prejudice when they have constant exposure and conversations with different groups of people.

The ability of diverse representation to inspire hope and ambition, and to serve as a catalyst for aspirations in under-represented groups holds so much weight when it comes to determining how many of these groups we actually see in the sporting industry.

We often come across the mantra that "it's hard to be what you do not see". This mantra emphasises the truth that people from marginalised and under-represented groups do not pursue careers in football or the sporting media if they have not seen a pathway toward it, much less knock on the door or even entertain the ideas to begin with. Positive media representation in these groups in the form of journalists, presenters, reporters and pundits places value on people of all backgrounds and increases their self-esteem. Football is not an exclusive group that caters only to a certain mould of individual. Footballers and those associated with the game from marginalised groups should not feel like they are trespassing. They should feel that it's a territory they are more than entitled to occupy with full transparency, assertiveness and a true sense of belonging.

A key cog in the efforts to spearhead diverse representation is consistency. Small disciplines and initiatives of seemingly insignificant impact done repetitively and relentlessly serve as stepping stones that lead to the ultimate goal: equity. Distinguished from equality—which is simply providing the same opportunity to all—equity acknowledges and adjusts the imbalances that place marginalised and under-represented groups at a disadvantage in the first place.

Being the first woman of colour to feature on the cover of a sports video game or the first homosexual male to captain a Premier League side would be commendable in isolation, but ultimately pointless in the long run if there are no efforts to address the systemic obstacles that prevent people from certain groups from succeeding in the first place.

An encouraging sight to witness in the past few years has been the collaborative effort of players, both former and active, in being more vocal about these social issues. The likes of Rio Ferdinand, Raheem Sterling and Marcus Rashford have had their say on the discrimination and racism toward black players, while current Chelsea Women's footballers Pernille Harder and Magdalena Eriksson have been a beacon of bravery and inspiration as role models within the LGBT community—prompting more conversations around being unapologetic about homosexuality, a topic that still remains taboo in the men's game.

In an interview with current Chelsea captain Cesar Azpilicueta on

The HangOUT show on Sky Sports News, Eriksson spoke out about some of the challenges she and her partner have faced, stating that "There is still that part of football where the fans contribute to a lot of hate and uncomfortable environments…" She further touched on how it has an impact on people choosing to attend matches, as well as other footballers not coming forward and being transparent about their homosexuality.

Extending beyond footballers themselves, content creators and freelance contributors within the sporting industry can also be commended on utilising their platforms and networks to hold individuals and social media platforms accountable for the way in which footballers of marginalised groups are treated and perceived.

Though great strides have been made in the bid to improve diversity, inclusivity and representation in the game, many would liken it to conquering one hill only to emerge on the other side and find that several more await.

In an interview with *The Athletic's* Roshane Thomas, former England and Manchester United player Rio Ferdinand highlighted how one of the challenges in combating issues of racism and inclusivity in football is getting footballers to speak up about their experiences. This should come as no surprise given the pushback and misconstrued coverage that players face when they are vocal about these issues. Players are often crippled and disheartened by the lack of support, empathy and assertive action that is taken in response to these issues, while others would prefer to not relive the trauma of their experiences through repeatedly sharing their stories.

The challenge is instilling bravery in players by encouraging them to cast off their coat of victimhood and using it to spearhead real change that will serve as a stepping stone for generations to follow. While there's a moment to acknowledge and lament the grievances we may harbour toward our transgressors, one way we may respond is through making the conscious decision to choose freedom, to choose change, and to commit to contributing toward such a key movement.

The traumas and setbacks that footballers, spectators and contributors experience as a result of belonging to a marginalised group cannot be quantified, nor is it qualitative. Yet the challenge remains to dare, yet again, to dream. Dream in the face of increasing shadows that threaten to be the sinister storytellers of misfortune. Dream even when it threatens to lead down the dark halls of disillusionment, disappointment and of despair. Dream while honouring, celebrating and commemorating your footballing peers and idols—you are not peering into the windows of someone else's story and hoping that their victories, failures or achievements add colour to your own. And most importantly—dare to overcome. More often than not, it may feel like one step is taken forward only to reel three steps back with the sucker punch of a setback, but in unity—in establishing an allied and unified approach to combat these issues as a collective front—the goal is all the more achievable.

Tokenism, microaggression and indifference

As much as the call for a collaborative effort is widely echoed, the fight for representation and inclusivity also calls for an approach that is intricate, delicate and discerning in nature. A failure to acknowledge and appropriately combat seemingly harmless actions like tokenism in boardrooms or microaggression among fellow supporters in stadium bleachers could prove more detrimental in the long run than one would assume.

In order to identify when diversity and authentic representation is achieved, the concept of tokenism needs to be defined and guarded against. Put simply, the distinguishing trait between the two is intention. While diversity acknowledges the unique traits that make us different—such as race, ethnicity, gender, sexual orientation and religious beliefs—and strives to foster a safe environment that explores these differences, tokenism merely engages in symbolic practices of being inclusive for the sole purpose of keeping up appearances. It is a hollow and insincere gesture that gives a public perception that diversity is an aspiration without actively working toward incorporating new ideas and perspectives into the status quo.

Engaging in acts of diversity and inclusivity under the mask of tokenism is not progressive. It only aims to appease the tension while conveniently avoiding the challenging conversations that will disrupt the dynamic and structure of the normally accepted practice. Footballers from marginalised groups within the sporting industry are sensitive to acts that involve them merely "ticking boxes" or "meeting a quota". They are further offended and discouraged when intentional measures aren't put in place to educate people and eradicate discrimination in the game.

Another seemingly unassuming threat to achieving diverse representation is being tolerant of microaggression. Microaggression includes subtle, offensive and unintentional statements or actions of discrimination toward marginalised groups. If they aren't called out, they contribute to the harmful nature of our social climate both within the bounds of football and beyond. The lack of awareness and cultural insensitivity toward issues regarding race, ethnicity, sexual orientation and religion only serve to leave negative lasting impacts on both professionals of the game, as well as supporters and others within the football industry in various capacities. The re-emerging antidote remains, once again—education. And the biggest threat to education? Indifference.

Indifference can be considered as far more of a threat to achieving diverse representation than ignorance might be. An individual who is ignorant possesses little to no knowledge of a particular matter, and hence holds no informed opinion.

By contrast, an individual who is indifferent maintains a passive stance even in light of information and awareness, making their indifference a conscious decision; a decision that inhibits the growth of the individual and the community with a silence so deafening that it only serves to drown out the indignant cries of injustice of the affected. While ignorance offers the opportunity that one could evolve and become an ally alongside the underrepresented through being open and receptive to information that may be challenging—but that is ultimately necessary and liberating—indifference acknowledges a reality yet conscientiously shuts the door on rectifying the issue. For example, societal issues that are prevalent in football through learned and misinformed prejudices. It would perhaps be deemed more of an honour to engage with ignorant individuals who are willing to overcome and revise their shortcomings, than those who maintain a persistent lack of care and concern through indifference.

Call to action

A reflection poses a series of all-important questions:
- Is the lack of affirmative action toward eradicating stereotypes and improving diversity and representation a societal issue?
- Should football claim responsibility for attempting to not only rectify the imbalances, but also spearhead positive and progressive efforts to expose, educate and eradicate the issues that contribute toward these imbalances?
- Should governing bodies and mere spectators of the game be expected to contribute more toward the beauty of the beautiful game in a wider capacity, beyond simply revelling in the spectacle itself?
- Should footballers remain indignant and persistent about demanding protection and accountability from the wider football community?

I believe the answers to these questions are as follows:
- The lack of affirmative action toward eradicating stereotypes and improving diversity and representation is a societal issue.
- Football can claim responsibility for attempting to rectify these imbalances, as well as commit to spearheading positive and progressive efforts to expose, educate and eradicate the issues that

contribute toward these imbalances.
- Governing bodies and spectators should aim to contribute more toward the beauty of the beautiful game in a wider capacity beyond simply revelling in the spectacle itself, as the football community is merely a society within society itself.
- Footballers should remain indignant and persistent about demanding protection and accountability from the wider football community. This could serve to trigger a ripple effect that will hopefully leave a lasting, positive impact for generations to follow.

We're all victims and/or witnesses of something—be it injustice, grief or disappointment. These misgivings of life can all stake a claim in our lives to some degree. Yet even amid these misgivings, life is gracious enough to grant us the option of free will—the ability to choose how we'll respond to the many questions life may ask us. Freedom is not a switch or quick setting that you merely activate on a whim—it is a journey that demands commitment, intention, patience and genuine desire. The journey is slow and gruelling, yet in the same breath it also proves to be worthwhile and rewarding. It comes at the cost of nothing but our comfort—because it is uncomfortable, but it is also freely accessible and there for the taking. Ultimately, it's a question of how badly do we want to see change?

Not one individual (nor I) can claim to hold a faultless formula that would rectify these challenges in one seamless move. Yet in my own experience as a marginalised individual (a young, black and foreign woman of Congolese nationality who's had to contend with the by-products of prejudices of my own), I can only commit to doing my small but significant part in spearheading change within the football industry and community that I love by being a voice and committing to education—both for myself and for others.

Rebecca Ngoie was born and raised as a Congolese national in South Africa and has recently moved to the US to study computer and information science in New York. She aims to work in information science while also pursuing her interest in writing. She would also like to run a non-profit centre to help women and children who have fallen victim to domestic violence. She is a passionate fan of the game and more specifically, Chelsea Football Club.

Football Fandom

by Luca Marie Wodtke

The fan community in football is one of the most important components of the sport. Supporters can both enjoy and be annoyed by the game, exchange ideas and talk to one another. But unfortunately, a good fan experience isn't open to all. Hate and resentment are still big parts of football fan culture. The discrimination suffered by females is significant. Misogyny is a constant companion for female fans, whether in the stadium, in social situations or online.

"Just because you are a woman, you know less."

"I [have] always loved football," Jùlia Belas said. The Brazilian national moved to the UK in January 2022 and currently works as a freelance writer for *The Guardian*. Jùlia grew up going to football stadiums with her mother in Salvador, and once the time came to apply for jobs, she knew she wanted to work in the field she loved.

When Jùlia experienced misogyny in the past, the comments were always aimed at her knowledge of the sport: "Most of the time, my opinion was neither heard nor validated. People assume that, just because you are a woman, you know less."

When she was young, the need to fit in was so strong that Jùlia would find herself engaging in misogynistic behaviour toward other female fans just to appease other spectators.

However, she believes there is less need for young female fans to do this nowadays as the overall situation has improved, and more females are accepted at football games: "While I was growing up, it was uncommon for women to show an interest in football. Now, there are women supporters' groups, families go together to games, and it is more common to see young girls liking football. However, there is still a lot of harassment and prejudice."

Jùlia hopes to see several improvements for females in football in the next few years: "Equal pay for players, financial incentives in grassroots women's football, more women—especially women of colour—being hired by the media and more women in coaching positions. There is more recognition and incentive, but there is also a lot more to do to continue to fight for equality."

"I would never go to a game alone."

A female fan, who wishes to remain anonymous for safety reasons and therefore will be referred to as "Alice", has experienced grave abuse online. Alice has been a football fan for over 20 years, and she says the most aggressive misogyny she has experienced is on social media.

The messages she receives vary, some being flirtatious and about her appearance. Alice said: "I find it quite intimidating when men message me like this—they often tell me they'll try to find me at games, and I've been asked whether I live alone. It makes me feel quite unsafe, and I would never go to a game alone because of this."

However, the latest messages Alice has been receiving are fuelled by hateful abuse about the fact that she is a female football fan. The only thing Alice wanted to do was to attend a match of her favourite team when an anonymous Twitter user insulted her in a vicious way. The perpetrator said he wished she would end up like Sarah Everard, a young British woman who was raped and murdered by a police officer in 2021, or for her to "be a woman [and] go and get [herself] assaulted". And these nasty comparisons were only because Alice is a female football fan.

It's not only hateful messages like this that scare Alice: "Misogynistic chants also make me feel very uncomfortable. The people singing them will rarely stop to think what they're saying, but when you're one of the few girls on a train home from a game, and everyone's chanting happily about sexual assault and abuse, it makes you feel very aware of yourself and your presence as a woman among a group of men. I can't join in with these chants.

"I find it harder to speak up in private interactions, like direct messages, than I do on my public social media feed," Alice said. To overcome this, she posted screenshots of the aforementioned abuse on her public Twitter feed. This felt "simultaneously more empowering and much safer".

Although her own experiences with misogyny have really impacted her life, Alice feels that the overall situation for females in football is improving: "Initiatives like 'Her Game Too' have given women and girls a platform and safe space for discussing their experiences of football, and I think this confidence has helped people like me speak up and challenge misogyny.

"The positive responses I received far outweighed abuse and criticism, and I came away from the experience surprisingly uplifted. There's a clear consensus that we need to make a stand against abuse of all kinds. More needs to be done to make football a normal experience for women, but I think most people are ready to confront that challenge.

"There are still major hurdles, including a culture of excessive drinking, and the persistence of offensive chants, which will take time and action to resolve, but I'm optimistic about the future—especially given the positive and supportive response my experience of abuse generated."

Alice has a few suggestions for how football can really improve: "The media can certainly do more. I had some good and some awful experiences with the media in the wake of my abuse. I was pressured to give personal information, including my surname and a photo of myself, in an article which cheapened and trivialised my experiences. Journalists should do more to support victims of abuse in all walks of life.

"On the field and within clubs, I'd like to see more women in backroom and managerial positions—this feels almost utopian, but there's no reason that a woman could not manage in men's football. Figures like Emma Hayes have helped generate discussion about the prospect of female managers in the men's game."

And finally: "Clubs can also do more to encourage women to attend. Doncaster Rovers have offered a financial incentive to women, but I think safety is a more pressing concern. Concrete reassurances about what women can expect from stewards and safety professionals, easily accessible information about how to report abuse and harassment, [as well as] promises that their voices will be heard would all be good incentives."

"It has affected my mental health."

Amy Fieldhouse-Downes attended her first Ipswich Town FC game at the age of 10 with her father: "Bless my Dad, having been teased relentlessly that three girls meant no one to go to the football with. Then he ended up with all three of us going, and football has stayed with me all my life."

After going to football games for over 25 years, Amy has had a range of experiences: "I do want to say that the vast majority of my life as a football fan has been positive, but I think the fact that most of us as women have experienced some form of sexism at football is why we have to stand up and talk about it right now."

"I've spent the last ten years or so on Twitter, and being quite an opinionated woman, this has placed me under the spotlight quite a lot for online abuse. Sometimes it's just been disagreements, and that's absolutely fine. But it very, very quickly turns personal, and when it does turn personal, it always goes against my gender. I cannot tell you how many times I've seen messages either sent directly to me or sent publicly, saying 'I feel sorry for her kids, she must be a terrible mother'; 'she shouldn't be a mother'. And this one was sent more recently, 'I feel sorry for her husband, can't believe anyone would marry that'."

The abuse Amy has faced online has ranged from patronising comments to very abusive words: "Don't talk to me like I'm a woman. Talk to me like I'm a football fan. I've had quite a lot of online bullying over the years, and it has affected my mental health massively, which is another reason I think it's really important to talk about the humans behind the screen."

Sometimes a lack of understanding can seem like misogyny, Amy noted: "There is definitely just blatant, awful sexist abuse. But at the other end of that scale is just underlying, unconscious bias. I'll be on the train to the football and people will be absolutely gobsmacked that I'm a woman going to the football and going on my own.

"I had a conversation with a Leeds Rhinos' fan. She said she went to games when she was younger because she went with her dad, but there was a period when she was a teenager when she didn't go because she couldn't—she was too old to go with her dad, but she didn't have a husband to take her. Then, when she had kids, she couldn't go because she had the kids to look after, so she was absolutely mind blown about the fact that I'm not only a woman going to games on her own, but that I'm a mum who goes to games. So for me, that signified the underlying bias that people have, and I do often get asked 'oh, what do you do with the kids?', which to me seems strange because you would never ask that of a man."

In person, Amy feels that she receives abuse less frequently compared to online. However, it does still happen: "I have had incidents of misogynistic behaviour, and the one that really stands out is when I was on my way home from a game. I was changing trains and I just sat down on the platform and these two blokes came over and we chatted, and they very sweetly asked if I was fine, and I said, 'oh yeah, thank you.' I thought, well, this is good. I've got people to be with, and I'm safe.

"So we were chatting away about football, and when we got on the train, I sat down with them. I told them I'm married. I told them I've got kids. We had a nice chat about that. And then, one of them leans over the table and kisses me right on the lips. I was just absolutely gobsmacked. His mate pulled him back gently, he didn't make a big deal out of it, but just said to him, 'that's out of order. Don't.' And the guy apologised, saying he was a bit drunk. So I sort of brushed it aside, but then he did it again. So, I caught the eye of an Ipswich fan and I said, 'oh wow, more Ipswich fans, I'm going to sit with them,' and they must've realised something was wrong, so they let me sit with them, only for a few more stops, but I was able to remove myself from a difficult situation.

"I think this is about safety and the fact that men just think they have this sort of superiority over us in that area, and that is what worries me," Amy said. "It's the toxic masculinity and the idea of their perception of superiority in the game. I honestly couldn't tell you how many times I've been pinched on the bum, either in the pub or at football on the concourse. It's not something that happens everywhere as an adult, it definitely is more pronounced at the football because of that being a male-dominated area."

Amy tends to speak out about the abuse she has endured online: "In person, I deal with the situation by stepping away. Online I deal with the situation by trying to talk to people calmly about it. Doesn't always work, and I will happily hit the block button for the worst offenders."

She has spoken about the incident with the man on the train on several occasions because to her, raising awareness is the best thing women can do for one another: "We are sharing examples of what is going on, to hopefully highlight the problem and so that for me is a really important thing of what we need to be doing, feeling safe within each other to share."

Not all the situations shared are met with support, however: "As soon as somebody shares something that's happened, yes, the vast majority of responses will be positive, saying it's wrong, and that includes men as well as women. But without exception, there are men in there saying she deserves it. I do speak out a lot online. It does get me a lot of negativity back, and it has affected my mental health in the past. I get hit with moments of anxiety going to games."

Despite all these experiences, Amy believes the situation is getting better for females in football: "I think when Dad first started taking me, it was quite unusual. The reason I didn't go until I was ten, I think was because I was a girl. It is definitely a lot better now and that is probably testament to the fact that it's a lot safer and a lot of football clubs are making sure that across the board, football is more inclusive, not just men and women but also people of all ethnicities.

"Things are improving every single day. I think with every generation that comes through, there's going to be more women that like football and that is going to help ease this gap that we have at the moment. Part of me thinks it's probably just something we need to wait for. We have shown how much difference we can make already, so let's keep that up."

Amy would like to see several improvements over the next few years: "I would like to see less men abusing women online. I would just like to see a bit more respect and that isn't just toward women, that is football fans in general on social media. They are really abusive toward each other. Football is all about opinions. But unfortunately, that leads to disagreements, and I think we as a generation, and as a digital generation, we probably all need to learn how to behave more politely, more compassionately on social media, and that includes toward women.

"Clubs need to find out what needs to be done. Ask your female fans. Find out what needs to be done and actually do something."

"Dad must have trained me well."

"I've loved football for as long as I can remember," Holly Scott said. She has been going to football games for over 13 years, attending her first Manchester United game at the mere age of five. "The United score dictates my mood, that goes for both the men's and women's teams."

Holly said she often experiences misogyny: "Whenever I wear a United top or go to Old Trafford, people make comments saying how my Dad or

Grandad force me to go, or how they must be disappointed that I'm a girl as that clearly means I love football less than men, which is completely untrue.

"It's the remarks of how 'my Dad must have trained me well' or that I 'know my stuff, for a girl,' not to mention the shocked looks on people's faces whenever I talk tactics, transfers and specific performances. Whenever I have a contradicting opinion, then I'm 'aggressive' or 'deluded', but a man can say the same thing and a sudden willingness to agree to disagree comes up."

Overall, Holly does believe that the situation for females in football is improving: "I think the emergence of prominent female footballers as pundits has greatly helped. There are a lot of male pundits who are purely employed because of their name—not on the basis of their football knowledge. These are slowly being replaced by women who know football inside out. I'm not too sure if there will ever be complete equality, but I can hope for the future."

Holly hopes to see a few improvements to empower females in the sport: "I wish to see women with knowledge of football hired to do footballing roles, and not just because they are women. I want to see more investment into women's football so that we can have more viable professional women's teams and a sustainable hierarchy. I want to see proper women's football academies.

"I want to see increased prize pots, so women's teams can afford to compete in their leagues and cup competitions and I also want to see women's teams have their own stadiums, as too often top teams in the WSL have to use non-league and lower-league stadiums which means that often games are called off due to conditions. I want female fans to be welcomed and just treated like the male fan base."

"No offence, love, but you'll never understand."

Brianna is originally from the United States and came to England to study at university: "I wanted to study media marketing and football, so I got [a] bachelor's degree in media studies. Being someone who was here to do my full degree, a lot of my tutors asked what brought me over here, and really it was football. When I finished, they encouraged me to go for my master's degree in football media and fan relationships, so I did that."

Currently, Brianna runs her own business, having moved away from working in football. She did work in the sport for a while: "I did a work placement for Liverpool Football Club, and then I actually worked for Everton. I worked in the community and that was quite rewarding in a sense. However, I worked with a lot of older people, and a lot of them were obviously big Everton fans and especially the older men definitely just disregarded anything that I had to say about the game."

The worst situation Brianna has experienced in the fandom was in a taxi in Liverpool: "The driver was saying, 'oh, you Americans call it soccer. Americans never understand the game and no offence, love, but you'll never understand it. You'll never understand the rivalries. You'll never understand the fan base.' I told him I was about to finish my postgraduate degree in football, and he just said, 'oh, OK,' and stayed silent. I think this hit me so hard because he was very adamant that I was incapable of understanding football.

"I have been accused of just watching football to watch men run around in shorts. I remember being in a pub once where I was wearing my Liverpool top. I was toward the back of the area that had the big screen and a guy stood in front of me and his mate said, 'oh hey, you know she can't see behind you,' and the guy looked at me, and he went back to his mate and he said, 'she's not watching anyway'."

Brianna believes social media culture plays a big role in the lack of equality between male and female fans: "I just want to go out there and just talk about the game while it's happening, or my own thoughts about the transfer window, but I feel maybe I don't hold as much weight as a girl who's prettier than me. I know that sounds awful, but sometimes I feel like that. I think people kind of pay more attention to the prettier football fans than the ones who are not on par with the male perception.

"Even with people like Alex Scott. She's utterly fantastic, but I just feel like it doesn't matter what comes out of her mouth because she is female and social media is so horrible. Men in particular are going to be quick to get on there and discredit her. I don't understand where they get off on that, honestly. You just go to the comment section on anything, and it's just awful, even recently. People don't really care what I have to say. It just doesn't seem to hold as much weight as if it was coming from a man."

When Brianna encounters misogyny, she has struggled to speak up for herself in the past: "I think places like the pub, I was still very quiet, and I think it was just more disbelief and not really knowing what to say. I don't want to say the wrong thing and then with my accent. I don't want to make things worse, so I think in those instances I was just quiet."

She does believe that a lot of the issues with misogyny in UK football come from the early years in the UK when girls are groomed to play netball in school rather than football, which is very different to the US. "My husband will talk to me about football, but when I ask if we should go out for a kickabout, he always declines. Apparently, it's unheard of here to have men and women playing together."

Overall however, Brianna can see football improving for the better: "I do think it's more OK to be a female football fan. The only problem is things like social media that can make it really difficult. I've not been to a game in a very long time, but the last few times I went, I was fine. Social media makes it hard. I think, 'should I put my opinion on Twitter?' But now I say, 'yeah, I'm just going to put it out there.'

"I think having women in leadership roles is important. Men are just going to have to realise just to chill out. There are some people who say, 'oh, I have these opinions strictly just because I prefer a male commentator's voice', and maybe that is true. I mean there is a bit of an uproar if it is a female commentator, an unnecessary uproar, but I do think that it does help, and I honestly do think having females in leadership roles in football does make a big difference."

"Football is more than a matter of life and death."

However, for these fans, there is still so much love for football.

For Alice, football is a way of escaping from daily life. "It's a healthy and welcome distraction from mundane things. Increasingly, it's been a way of making friends—social media has been wonderful for this. Recently, it's been a means of personal and collective empowerment for me. 'Her Game Too' asked me to be an advocate for them in the wake of my abuse, and it's been fantastic to have a group of girls to talk about all aspects of the game with, who will back me up if I experience any further harassment."

Football also plays a huge role in Holly's life: "it's the way I connect with so many of my loved ones, from my Dad and Grandad right through to my best friend, with whom I formed a close bond through football. The scores that week affect what mood I'm in, and I spend unbelievable amounts of money to watch and support my team."

Brianna only started watching football because a friend told her to watch a Liverpool game: "what really captivated me was that everyone was singing. People are singing, and they're holding up scarves—I didn't understand. I watched it more and more and just fell in love with it so much."

Now, football plays a huge role in her life: "I met my husband through football. It's really enjoyable. I love being part of a community of other football fans. We all have our different opinions on how it should be run or this player and that player, and that performance of that game and everything. But at the end of the day, we all love Liverpool. Well, until you get comments about how you can never understand because you are a woman."

For Jùlia, football is her work, her personal life and her activism. She said: "it is part of some of the highs and lows of my life. I am passionate about it and I think I always will be."

"I got married last summer," Amy said, "and my Dad's speech began with 'when you think of Amy, you think of football'. Football is a huge part of my life, to the point where my husband has a running joke about where he stands in my priorities. Football doesn't come first of course, like you have to balance out, and you have to pick your family life first and your career first and things like that. But football is hugely, hugely important to me. And I will go to great lengths to be able to be a part of this world."

Amy has travelled across the country to support her club, including a drive from Yorkshire to Ipswich to watch the game where the 'Her Game Too' campaign was introduced to the club. "It's the only thing I have felt this passionate about for this long in my life. This isn't just a fad. This isn't just something silly. This is a passion for me. I would not be me if I wasn't a football fan."

For Amy, the words of former Liverpool manager Bill Shankly echo what football means to her. "Football is more than a matter of life and death. That's what it is for me. I always believed that. I could never see anything coming first over football. I joke of course, my kids do [come first]. But because football means so much to me, I have found a way to get a good balance between loving my family and loving my club.

"For my whole life, they are the only thing in the world I know will still be there when I reach the end of my life too. So, they are my true love," Amy said.

Luca Marie Wodtke is from Stuttgart, Germany. She completed her tertiary education in England where she has lived since 2016. Lucy works as a content strategist with an advertising company, having previously co-founded a website to advise young people on a career in football.

Virtual Turnstiles: Barriers to Entry and Technological Gatekeeping in Women's Football

by Caroline Stefko

Women's football is on the cusp of a period of rapid growth, straddled between successful regional tournaments in 2022 (the UEFA Women's Euro, the Concacaf W Championship and the Women's Africa Cup of Nations) and the 2023 Women's World Cup. Interest in the women's game has never been greater; attendance records have been shattered in matches ranging from domestic leagues to international friendlies, and there has also been an increase in media coverage to meet the demand for analysis and punditry around showcase fixtures. In theory, the future for women's football should be looking very bright.

Yet the impact of this fresh excitement has not been distributed uniformly among the various domestic leagues, nor even among individual teams within those leagues. While a match between Arsenal and Tottenham continues to set new Women's Super League (WSL) attendance records with each iteration of the local derby surpassing 40,000 fans, a relegation scrap between Leicester and Reading might barely draw 2,000. The league's average attendance obscures the reality that some teams are drawing much larger crowds than others.

This disparity can also be seen online when comparing social media engagement for different teams within a league, as well as by comparing engagement between a club's women's team and its men's team (assuming that any given club has a women's team—still not a given at all levels of the football pyramid in many countries). In fact, there are times when the majority of replies to a tweet about a women's team match is flooded with comments from disgruntled fans of the men's team.

As a fan of teams on both sides of the 'pond' (the Atlantic Ocean), I can't always speak to the reality of the match-going experience and where improvements could be made to increase attendances (ticketing, stadium amenities, pricing, etc.). But I do have firsthand experience of the many barriers to entry on the technological side of things. These barriers either discourage people from becoming new fans or hinder their deeper engagement with women's football teams and leagues, both near and far. There are many factors unique to the women's game that can make following football difficult for a modern, global fan.

Broadcasting

The obvious starting place of inquiry is the state of broadcasting for women's football. In today's world, that is more likely to involve streaming than a television broadcast, though the latter plays into the equation at times, and to varying degrees based on where a fan is tuning in from. For example, from my home in the United States, I can access legal streams for the majority of the European women's domestic leagues, but the WSL is the only league occasionally shown on actual television broadcasts here. Even the United States' own domestic league, the National Women's Soccer League (NWSL), is rarely televised—let alone in prime time. In one infamous instance, the 2021 NWSL final (hosted in Louisville, Kentucky) had a local kick-off time of noon ET. Unbelievably, this was an improvement over the originally scheduled plan to hold the final in Portland with a local kick-off time of 9am to accommodate the only available broadcast slot on CBS. Sometimes, working around unrealistic expectations from television broadcasters is more trouble than it's worth.

Furthermore, streams for these leagues are often spread across several different platforms, and some of those exclusively cater for women's football. They therefore are not platforms that many consumers already subscribed to before discovering an interest in women's football, nor platforms that are seen as good value for money through having a variety of sports and/or leagues in their other offerings. In men's football, fans also often have to subscribe to multiple streaming platforms to be a 'completist' and watch all of a team's possible matches, but the matches are at least on more well-known and popular platforms to begin with and offer a better value for the subscription fee by providing access to multiple leagues and competitions. The siloing of women's football can discourage crossover interest from existing fans of the men's game who are already at streaming subscription saturation.

To dig into a specific example of a streaming platform that exclusively hosts women's football, let's take a look at The FA Player. It includes access to the WSL and the second-tier Championship, as well as the two domestic cup competitions in England and bonus content about the England women's national team. The major advantage of watching matches on The FA Player is that they are free. However, the selection is limited; certain matches are only available to watch via television broadcast in the UK or with one of the league's overseas broadcasting partners (possibly another streamer) in other parts of the world, so a subscriber would miss a few matches every season by relying just on The FA Player for access.

The difference in production quality between the matches selected for streaming and the matches selected for broadcast can be staggering. The more prestigious matches shown on the traditional broadcasts often have full pre-game, halftime and post-game shows, while matches only shown on The FA Player have extremely limited punditry and analysis. The FA Player opts instead to show pre-recorded highlight clips or special programming during the halftime interval. Some of that content isn't relevant to fans of all teams. The quality of commentary can also vary widely between the two different broadcast types. Then there are the frequent streaming glitches on The FA Player and the lack of a native app for televisions to ensure a seamless streaming experience (but at least there is a mobile app).

While the traditional broadcasts of women's football evoke the full spectacle of a top-flight match like a broadcast of the men's Premier League, the streamed matches can seem rather lacklustre by comparison. If I were a WSL executive hoping to showcase the league to its best advantage, I know which platform I would prefer to have a new or prospective fan experience for their first match. Ideally, watching a game should be an effortless and immersive activity, and that is simply not the case when it comes to The FA Player.

To share one more example of the limitations of the platforms that exclusively stream women's football, consider ata football, known as the global home of women's football. In many parts of the world, ata football is the only platform that offers legal streaming for some of the European leagues, like the Frauen-Bundesliga in Germany and Liga F in Spain. The problem is that on any given match day, ata football only has the rights to show a select number of matches. They are generally ones involving the teams at the top of the league tables. So, if you're a fan of a team lower down the table, it's unlikely you'll be able to see many of their matches over the course of the season. And like The FA Player, ata football is plagued with technical glitches that can make streaming a match a frustrating (and sometimes futile) experience. However, unlike The FA Player, ata football requires a paid subscription to unlock access to live matches. With that membership you gain perks like broadcasts with halftime analysis and more professional commentary, but you are still limited by which matches are offered.

It's a balancing act no matter which streaming platform a league strikes a partnership with. Some have better production values, some have more reliable streaming quality, and some win by sheer virtue of quantity over quality. But at this point in time, it doesn't matter which league or team you prefer to watch, it will always be a stressful task trying to figure out where to watch a game on any given day—and then you have to hope the broadcast is functioning.

Engagement opportunities outside of games

Being able to actually watch the matches is only half of the problem. The next step in becoming a true fan of women's football is engaging with the sport outside of games, whether by talking to other fans about the results and players, enjoying content from other fans like podcasts and blogs, or playing fantasy football, just to name a few options. I'll address each of them in turn, as each has its own corresponding issues.

One has to be able to find other fans first in order to have a conversation with them, especially if you don't have the benefit of going to games in-person and easily meeting like-minded fans.

There are a few websites/apps that are popular as gathering places: Twitter, Tumblr and Discord (listed in order of the most unrestricted to the most exclusive). The sad truth is that fans of women's football face harassment in all of these spaces, although it is less of an issue on Discord which is made up of individual servers that are typically invite-only and therefore less likely to be filled with hostile internet trolls.

Twitter and Tumblr's search functions enable a lot of "bot"-like behaviour from users who go looking for a fight—and there are a lot of people, primarily men, who choose to spend their time raining on the parade of anyone who expresses excitement (or any kind of feeling, really) about women's football. As mentioned previously, this is often a side-effect of fans looking for an outlet to express their frustration or disappointment around a club's men's team. Taking that resentment out on other fans trying to mind their own business in conversations about women's football is an everyday occurrence; you would be hard-pressed to find a single women's football fan existing in any capacity online that hasn't received or witnessed this kind of harassment. It can be very demoralising trying to build a community of fans around a women's team only to have interlopers with bad intentions disrupting the peace.

On the opposite end of the spectrum, we go from harassment to being completely ignored. This is a familiar emotion for fans of women's football teams that aren't particularly popular or successful, whether historically or in the present. It can be difficult to find fan content (or even professional punditry and analysis) that covers those kinds of teams unless it is from a team-specific outlet. Podcasts, newsletters and YouTube channels that cover the leagues with a general focus usually give short shrift to all but the most-established teams, sometimes unconsciously. This is problematic, because those same successful teams continually get the lion's share of media coverage and it becomes a perpetuating cycle. Teams that benefit from this free word-of-mouth find it easier to attract new fans because they are seen as prestigious and prosperous. The more fans they attract, the more their match-day revenues increase, and the more entrenched they become at the top of the standings through investment in their player squads. All the while, teams at the bottom of the table have to fight for media scraps.

In fairness, this problem exists in men's football as well, but more so on the professional media side of things. Even the unluckiest of mid-tier men's teams have established fan bases by now and can count on a consistent network of fan content to maintain support through difficult times on the pitch. For many women's teams, those fan media networks simply do not exist, or are only beginning to put down their foundations. It can be a lonely place for those content creators until a critical mass finally joins and challenges the status quo of the top teams.

Fantasy football is perhaps the most interesting case of fan engagement, since it is a game itself. Fans who play fantasy football are some of the most knowledgeable and passionate fans out there, and they are consistent in their engagement since there are actual deadlines involved with picking their players, making transfers and checking leader boards. People who enjoy the highs of celebration and the lows of commiseration get a double dose of those emotions through the outcomes of their fantasy teams, and it's another avenue for bonding with like-minded fans.

The problem is that many (I would hazard a guess and say the majority) of women's football leagues across the world don't have corresponding fantasy leagues. The websites that host fantasy leagues are finally starting to cotton on to the appeal of women's fantasy football and have leagues for a few of the top-flight divisions. There was also a lot of hype around fantasy football during recent Euros, and it will surely be a possibility for the upcoming World Cup. But women's fantasy football leagues aren't advertised as widely as those for men's leagues. It's another missed area of opportunity to help fans to learn more about the players they watch every week and have some friendly competition with fellow supporters.

Finally, there is a dearth of information and education around women's football overall. Things that you often take for granted as a fan of men's football, like adequate score-notification apps, are woefully inadequate in the women's football market. Some of the most popular score apps don't even have women's leagues as options to track, or if they do, the information is incomplete or out of date. I personally use the FotMob app and appreciate its many innovative features, but I have noticed that some data is incomplete for the women's leagues that I track. The "transfers" tab is one that I utilised heavily this past summer to keep abreast of updates in the men's transfer market, but that feature isn't an option yet for the women's leagues. There are even players in certain squad lists that have been retired since before the start of the season, so in that regard the app is way behind the curve.

Popular statistics' websites are also guilty of this unequal attention between men's and women's players, not just on mobile apps like FotMob but also on browser-only sites like FBref. Certain advanced stats are only available for men's leagues and players, and it limits the amount of analysis that can be done, making media coverage shallower on the women's side. Progress is being made, but the fact that women's football was completely banned in many countries until the not-so-distant past means that there is a limited amount of historical data as well. Such staples of football history as websites logging "head-to-head" records between teams are only now starting to be created for many women's teams.

Even something as simple as a match-day report can look vastly different for a men's fixture compared to a women's fixture. Sky Sports' website is a resource I use frequently in my own research, and their match reports have two- to three-times as much detail for a men's fixture as they do for a women's fixture (and even then, only if it's a match involving one of the top-of-the-table teams—other fixtures are lucky to have anything more than the scoreline and key events, let alone an accompanying highlights video or mention of who earned the player of the match award). All of these little things add up to make the possibilities for historical analysis of women's football far too limited.

I won't touch on the topic of betting too much due to ethical concerns, but this is another area in which demand is currently not being met for women's football. Betting can undeniably be a source of camaraderie between fans, as well as a gateway to being a broader fan of whole leagues, as opposed to just one specific team within a league—a breadth over depth approach, if you will.

Investment

This brings me to the most crucial driver in reducing all of these barriers to experiencing women's football: investment. There has to be increased buy-in from the relevant stakeholders; from league sponsors to broadcast networks to the more visible participants in the match-day economy (like score apps, fantasy football leagues, etc.). The technological infrastructure for women's football must be improved immediately—and continually—lest the current potential for growth be squandered. It's particularly important for fans interested not only in their local leagues, but also in the wider international game. Men's football has long benefitted from this global interest, and the women's game should too.

There is plenty of reason for optimism that progress is being made. Gaps are being filled every day as new investment flows in. Fans of women's football are being recognised as true priorities by sports media markets and broadcasters alike. Part of this upward trend has been sparked by the increased number of retired women's footballers who decide to keep working in the football industry in some capacity—whether as pundits or coaches or by enabling the expansion of domestic leagues as investors or team executives. As we have seen particularly in the NWSL, sometimes you have to build the things that you want to see. And these retired players understand that although it's usually a pure love of sport that initially draws viewers into watching women's football, it takes a superior match-day product to keep them watching and keep them coming back. As leagues across the world continue to become more professionalised and operate at higher standards, they will be able to move past the growing pains caused by creating these kinds of infrastructure, both physical and digital, from scratch. You don't necessarily have to reinvent the wheel that is men's football. You can learn from its mistakes and make the women's wheel turn more smoothly.

Just as the shortage of resources and the scarcity mindset within women's football media has perpetuated some negative cycles (like the entrenched dominance of a few select teams), there is some potential for developing positive cycles by creating both professional and fan-media spaces that are inclusive and comprehensive right from the start. Lessons can also be learned when it comes to the at-times toxic nature of discourse around men's football. Women's football would perhaps like to shed the image of being solely a family-friendly match-day environment, but it would do well to foster a more welcoming environment—both in stadiums and in places where fans gather online.

Demand for women's football feels like it is at its peak, but it's only getting started from the grassroots level to the professional leagues. Fans will come if you let them.

The key will be in ensuring that these new fans feel valued and are catered for in the same way that fans of men's football have been for decade upon decade. Fans of women's football deserve to have their curiosity and passion respected. They also don't deserve having to make concessions or compromises when it comes to something as basic as watching their favourite team's matches. By removing technological barriers to women's football, it will be able to thrive.

Caroline Stefko from San Antonio, Texas. She is a podcaster and newsletter writer passionate about making football content accessible to all types of fans. She covers Tottenham Hotspur's men's and women's teams from San Antonio, Texas, and writes from a global fan perspective. She would like to write more about the intersection between football and politics.

Racism in Women's Football

by Francesca Lever

Picture the scene. England have just won the Women's Euro 2022. It was the first major title for any English team in 56 years. It is a running joke in my family that the previous win was nine months before my mother was born. Wembley had a record attendance of 87,192 for the final of Women's Euro 22. The crowds were singing *Sweet Caroline* so loud. It was a perfect moment. Nothing could replace the feeling or top the experience.

But there had been whispers during the whole competition. People who had followed the sport for a while were aware of the issue but new fans were asking and wondering *"why are most of the players white?"* During what should have been England's brightest hour, there was a cloud over their success.

Only three of 23 players in the English squad were people of colour–Jess Carter, Nikita Parris and Demi Stokes–but they barely featured in the starting XIs. By way of contrast, 15 of 23 players of quarter-finalists France were of colour.

You could argue that race is irrelevant, but nonetheless the question has to be raised: do players of colour get the same opportunities as their white counterparts?

The whiteness of the England team may come as a surprise to some, because black women have held visible roles in English women's football and continue to do so. Hope Powell was the first woman to coach England and continued her career managing Brighton & Hove Albion until recently. Alex Scott and Eniola Aluko work in football commentary following successful playing careers.

In November 2022, one of the England team's leading stars, Beth Mead, said in response to a question about whether there was "an obvious explanation or is it just coincidental" for the team to have few black women: "I think it is completely coincidental. We put out our best 11 and you don't think of anyone's race or anything like that. I think that's more an outsider perspective."

Mead's comments were met with strong criticism online. Donald McRae, *The Guardian* journalist who conducted the interview, later confirmed that it "was a clumsy way of asking whether there could be any alternative reason to systemic racism."

Two of Mead's teammates (Leah Williamson and Lotte Wubben-Moy) had other answers when asked about racism and opportunities for young players of colour. Williamson said: "We don't ever want anybody to feel like it's not their game, because of the way they look or the colour of their skin. We would be devastated if we felt like we were contributing to that."

Wubben-Moy added: "I'm not going to sit here and say I feel any hardship. I'm white, I have such a massive privilege and I acknowledge that, which is part of the reason why I feel like I have such a responsibility also to push for more change to allow young, black, Asian [or] any child to be able to see someone like them playing football. You've got to see it to believe it."

Grassroots

The problem starts at grassroots football. Research shows that racism has been and still is embedded in both men's and women's football in England.

The England female scouting system lacks the needed people on the ground, the needed resources and the ability to look further. There is no denying that the ability and talent of the England players is untouchable and that the coaches have a selection of mainly white players. By the time you are at senior and international duty, it is overwhelmingly clear. There is not as much diversity across the leagues as there should be.

This fact should not discredit the English women's success at all. But it is an issue that needs highlighting and looking at from every aspect. The UK is full of people of different colours; it is impossible to believe that all (or nearly all) the best players are white.

It can be argued that demographics in areas of the country come into play. For example, the North East is much 'whiter' than other areas. Even so, scouts do not seem to identify those in more diverse areas. Why is that? Are they not looking in the right places, or is it the case that they cannot be bothered to look?

In an in-depth look into the issue in relation to women's football, former player Anita Asante claimed it could be the set-up of the Women's Super League that could be contributing toward the lack of diversity. She said that when it first started, the clubs involved were more diverse but as time went on, they became less so.

One of the reasons is that training grounds moved from cities and towns to the countryside. It is becoming more and more common for women's teams to train in similar places as their counterpart male clubs, but because there is not as much money in women's football, struggling black families might not be able to afford to send their children to training grounds. The male teams will pay for players' transport from school and home, but the same service is not offered to the female teams—so young black players often miss out. In the Premier League, young players are often housed with host families to make sure they have home comforts and every opportunity, but there is no similar support for the Women's Super League players.

It is wrong to assume that all black families are in this situation, the same as it is wrong to assume all white families can afford to send their children to training, but the data shows that more young black female players are missing out.

Another issue is that schools are slow or hesitant to offer football as an option in physical education.

Asante said that during her career she never worked with a non-white coach, apart from Hope Powell, so the issue also goes beyond just playing.

Women's Euro 2017

It is also important to mention that black players may be discouraged by the events of Women's Euro 2017 when black forward Eni Aluko alleged that England manager Mark Sampson had made direct, racist comments to her during the time she was in the team. There was a serious chain reaction of events after the allegation was made. Firstly, Aluko was not believed. Secondly, a goal celebration that included Sampson led by black forward Nikita Parris in the next match after the allegation led to Aluko criticising the players involved and accusing them of selfishness and a lack of respect. She was a media commentator at the event and argued that they required diversity training. Thirdly, right-back Lucy Bronze (a white English player) questioned whether Aluko was even good enough to be in England's squad. Aluko expressed her surprise and disappointment over the lack of support from England players. Sampson was later sacked after a Football Association (FA) investigation into Aluko's allegations.

It is important to note that Parris has since apologised for the goal celebration, calling it a "thoughtless action" that lacked empathy and understanding, and she also claimed that it showed ignorance. In addition, an investigation conducted by the Football Association uncovered evidence of Aluko's own negative behaviour, including the assault of another player during her time with the England team.

Regardless of where you stand in relation to these events, they would likely leave black players with questions and concerns on how they would be treated in the football profession.

On the flip side, people have argued: so what if all the English players are white if they are getting the results? They represent a good proportion of young girls dreaming of football glory. We have seen these English players fighting from a young age to have a place in the football world. From lack of facilities to sexism, they still suffer to an extent. It is a difficult balance to get right because you do not want to discredit their efforts, but it is still extremely important to raise awareness of any racist issues.

Some could argue: why can't we just cheer on our team without bringing anything else into it?

In 2021 when the men's team made their own Euro final, they lost the game on penalties. Three young black players in the England team were then subject to racist abuse online. However, their 2018 World Cup squad did include 11 players of colour, while the following year for the Women's World Cup, only two were called up.

FA diversity programs

The Football Association is trying though. They have developed schemes that include replacing regional talent centres with a more accessible network of up to 70 emerging talent centres funded by the Premier League for girls aged eight to 16.

Also, there is 'Discover My Talent', a program set up by the FA and supported by Sport England that enables anybody—coaches, parents, teachers or youth club workers—to refer any player to England's talent pathway. It operates over five regions.

The Professional Footballers' Association has also launched a new campaign named '#SeeItAchieveIt' Its aim is about increasing diversity representation in the women's game.

Sadly, none of these initiatives adequately tackle the way non-white women and girls are treated in football.

Kay Cossington, FA's head of women's player development and talent, told *She Kicks* magazine in 2020 that "inclusivity was compromised as we attempted to turn more professional", adding "we had 52 centres of excellence; that was too many for the depth of talent at the time".

Those 52 centres were reduced to 30, with many in rural areas—but the FA said its new 'emerging talent centres' approach has 60 centres, close to its target of 70 and that it is making "a very positive picture". An FA spokesperson said the new program will engage with approximately 3,810 players—a 92% increase on the 1,722 players under the old pathway.

Visibility

Visibility remains one of the biggest issues. During Euro 2022, a discussion about racism led by Eilidh Barbour led to backlash on the internet. It was made out she was criticising the squad selection, but it could also suggest that people are in denial about the problem.

Barbour commented that the all-white 'Lioness' squad in 2022 would "stop black girls from dreaming" of being professional footballers. She stated: "It was a historic eight-goal victory for England last night as the Lionesses secured their place in the quarter-finals. But all starting 11 players and the five substitutes that came on to the pitch were all white. And that does point toward a lack of diversity in the women's game in England."

In response, the BBC were labelled as 'woke' for airing the comments. Some questioned the relevance and significance of the comments, claiming that there was nothing wrong with the Lionesses being all white if they were the best players.

Fellow commentator Emily Hewertson said that she felt sorry for England women's coach Sarina Wiegman, who she said simply "can't win." She tweeted : "If they for example started Nikita Parris, one of the less in-form players in the squad, and England proceeded to lose that match, I am sure BBC commentators would be criticising the manager's strange choice to start her."

Hewertson then highlighted that there was not a single white woman selected to represent Team England in the 100-metre, 200-metre and 400-metre events at the 2022 Commonwealth Games.

In a column for *MailOnline*, Dan Wootton said: "No wonder we're turning off the woke BBC in droves when they're using our brilliant football Lionesses to stoke racial divisions." He continued: "Is the BBC suggesting national sporting teams should now have ethnic quotas? Or do they have evidence of systemic racism within women's football? If so, they should investigate and produce evidence before broadcasting. More likely, this was just yet another attempt to try and paint England as institutionally racist, when the Sewell Report concluded conclusively that is not the case."

In 2019, former footballer and pundit Claire Rafferty commented on racism within the game. She said it would be naive to say that racism does not exist and that it is important to educate people.

Her comments came during the same year as former player Sophie Jones retired from football after being found guilty of racism during a game. It was said that she made monkey noises toward another player—something which Jones denies. She retired after saying she did not have faith working under the FA. She said she does not condone any form of racism.

Goalkeeper Aman Dosanj signed for Arsenal's Academy when she was 16 years old. In 1999, she became the first British South-Asian player to represent England at any level, playing in an Under-16s tournament.

She says she experienced racism throughout her career, ranging from microaggression to racial slurs. "You need to remember that regardless of whether you're on a football pitch, or away wherever you are, our race enters a room before we do. I can see why so many parents are scared to put their kids into that kind of hostile environment."

Representation is so important everywhere, including in football. Action is too. Young girls want to see women performing at the highest level. Whether it is someone of colour or just a woman in general, it is key to see that.

The England women's squad still took the knee as a sign of respect and solidarity before playing when their male counterparts had stopped doing so. Demi Stokes has said to the *Evening Standard* that it is very important to keep doing the gesture because the players are sick of getting racial abuse. She said it needs to be done all the time "not just for Black History Month". She has been the victim of abuse online like many other black players. She also commented that because of the abuse, she has constant performance pressure because she knows what will happen if she misses a penalty.

Stokes also wrote a letter to her eight-year-old self which is available on her club's (Manchester City's) website. She wrote about the racism that would happen in her life, and about being from a mixed raced family and the abuse that would come with that. How when she was called names, she would get into fights. She had to make sure that did not spill into her games or she would be sent off.

We need to hear more stories and letters like this.

Stokes now has a platform to raise awareness and be a role model. "Not everyone is comfortable but you don't have to be black to speak about black issues. It does not matter whether you are black or white. It comes down to what's morally right and wrong," she said in her letter.

This is something that strikes a chord with me. I am a white person and it does feel hypocritical sometimes to be so passionate about an issue that will never affect me personally. It is also an issue where I am guilty by association.

Because women's football is treated as a second-class sport, it is going to have a knock-on effect on the equality issues already happening. So, it is important across the board that those who have the automatic privilege use their platform to raise awareness of the issues, and be allies for the BAME (black, Asian and minority ethnic) community.

The current stats are: 43% of players currently playing men's Premier League are black, while in the female equivalent, the Women's Super League, this falls to less than 10% (29 players out of a total of 300).

Sapphire McIntosh grew up playing in Leeds United's youth teams. She says watching the England team at the Euros reminded her of playing at

Leeds when she was younger. She said: "I was the only black girl in the U-16s development squad. I wasn't made to feel comfortable. [The Euros] just reminded me of playing footy there. Even at university, that's pretty much how it always looked, like the England women's team."

McIntosh said during her first year at Leeds, none of the other players talked to her, but she continued playing out of sheer love for the game, despite it taking "bravery".

Growing up, she was a huge Rachel Yankey fan, but said now there are fewer players to inspire girls of colour, making the sport less relatable for them. "I don't really know if I look at the England women's team and go 'oh, this is me, this is inspiring'. That's not really where I get my inspiration."

The fight for equality is going to be a long one. But it is a very important one and everyone needs to be on board.

Football is for everyone—not just a select group. Work needs to start from the bottom up. It is easy to look at the England squad with a critical eye but they have every right to be there too—they just need to use that platform, not be naive to what is happening, and always be vocal.

Sexist and racist abuse, as well as images of whiteness and the difficulties of calling out racism, may deter the next generations of players. If football is indeed a "game for all", it must commit to diversity throughout the sport: from player development in schools through the structures of the game to the very top.

Francesca Lever from Manchester has a masters in sports journalism and is currently working as a freelancer principally with the BBC. Her goal is to be a sports journalist with a focus on football.

Fiction

Sidelines

by Olivia Barber

Mae looked out over the playing field, tracing the gleaming blades of grass among the balding patches of claggy mud. The sky was a dim grey and the moist air weighed down. The fresh-faced adolescents floated across the pitch in formation–a pass forward, a yell at the running midfielder, the ball quickly expelled to a striker, a command to shoot. The boys' square shoulders and puffed-out chests occupied the local school field like comical clones of footballers they'd seen on television.

Mae's brother Nick, the team's most prolific goals scorer, led the charge. When Nick first started playing at age seven, Lily would drag Mae along. She was a small child and Lily could not leave her at home. At 14, the sidelines were still as far as she went, yet Mae never considered herself a spectator. Mae pictured herself twirling around with the ball toward her team's shooting end, weaving it through gaping feet, retrieving it and firing it into the net. She flung her arms in the air like an aeroplane that had a broad, toothy grin for propellers. Then the boisterous shouts of the dads, the smell of boys sucking on orange segments and the 'spitty' speeches about second-half tactics disrupted her dreams. "Mae, did you hear me? We need to rush off after this, I've got to get to work," Lily warned, her voice giving off the sound of an abrasive alarm clock. Mae gave an automated nod.

The referee announced three minutes of extra time. Mae dropped her gaze and scanned her worn trainers. She pictured her feet moving silkily doing tricks. Turns. The dance. The shrill final whistle sounded. Lily grasped the edge of Mae's coat sleeve, ushering her toward the gate where the crowds of bleating children guided by their weary parents were also heading. "I'll just go and say goodbye to Nick," Lily said. She jogged over to Nick, said "well done!" and walked away. Nick looked briefly at Mae and then turned away to his huddling teammates. As Lily strode on, Mae cleared her throat and demanded, "Mum, when do I get to play?"

Lily scrutinised her daughter's face as though she only faintly recognised her, having not looked at her properly for a long time.

"I don't know, there isn't a girls' football team around here and I can't be ferrying you across the county," Lily replied.

"So why can Nick play? Are you saying it's a boy's game?" Mae responded, slowing to look back at the pitch. Maybe she'd find the answer on the field or in one of the boys' faces.

"Your bus is at three minutes past, mine is the one after. Let's get moving," Lily said.

"You didn't answer. Why can he play, but I can't?" Mae asked.

"Because he has a team and there isn't one for you! We can't miss this bus," Lily announced, distracted as ever by timekeeping and bus schedules. Everything was a task to complete and the burden of responsibility weighed heavily on her. They'd spent the last 105 minutes watching Nick's match, plus the bus there and back. *Was that out of responsibility or because Lily cared?* Mae wondered, a twang of heat rushing to her throat.

Lily paced ahead toward the bus stop, gaining half a dozen strides on Mae. Mae's cheeks stung and her breath was shallow and rapid.

As Lily approached the bus stop, Mae shouted ahead, "I'm walking!"

"The bus leaves in two minutes, just come here and wait with me," Lily said. Her face looked washed out with tiredness, even at a distance.

"So you won't let me walk either?" Mae asked as she caught up with her mum.

"Mae, please, it'll go dark soon. I worry. You know I'd take you home but I have to get to my shift." Lily's voice was faint, her darkened eyes pleading.

Mae knew why her mother worried about her walking home in the dark.

It niggled at Mae when her mother made inferences and coded warnings. She'd plant fears, but she wouldn't own up to them being hers, and a guessing game inevitably followed.

"You're talking about Aimee, aren't you?" Mae pointed out.

Lily looked at her phone. "We might be working late tonight, they want us to clean St Leonards and Branwood."

When the '75' bus rolled in later than the timetabled slot, Mae said goodbye to Lily and clambered on, holding her pass up to the driver through the smudged screen. The bulky man, slouched as if part of his seat, barely looked at the photo card and then bobbed his head. "Cheers now."

Mae found herself an empty window seat at the front of the bus and turned her body 45° to look out. The streets were calm. A family rambled back from their Sunday walk, chattering and smiling, two boys on bikes dropped their shoulders over the handlebars as they raced each other, and Ava, one of Mae's school friends, was walking her dog with her mum. Mae placed her bony elbow on the window and put her hand over her eyes. She needed to get off the bus.

Her feet stomped one, two as they met the pavement. Mae put her head in her hood to form a cocoon and started walking toward the corner shop. Her heart pounded and she sharply inhaled to try and steady herself. Tears flowed down to her chin, rolling down the curve to her neck. An ugly orange glow shone down on the dark grey streets and the droplets on Mae's face. Semi-detached houses lined up with brightly coloured doors, their front room lights casting soft light onto the street, and their large TVs lit up with the evening news.

Mae veered off down the side street to her house. The smell of frying onions and boiling vegetables were in the air. After the strip of larger houses with high hedgerows, Mae reached the narrow path leading to her estate. She filed down the path to the play area. The playground equipment was empty. There were no children playing on the swings or flinging themselves down the slides. In the corner, a group of boys had dumped their bags and bikes down and were kicking a ball between them. Boys whose parents, teachers, coaches not only let them play football, but cheered them on, saw the pitch as their place, and afforded them the freedom and joy of play. They were friends of Nick's, one of them was Sean, Damian's little brother. He was in Mae's school year. Mae slowed down, looking on from behind the railings, still ensconced in her hood.

One of the taller boys booted the ball, funnelling it between the posts holding up the climbing frame tower. "GOALLLLL!!!" He roared. Another boy groaned and bounced along to collect the ball. It was wedged beside the railings where Mae stood.

As he stood up, he saw Mae. "Are you… watching us?" he asked with a chuckle, revealing a gap in his teeth. "Lads, we've got a supporter!" he shouted over to the cluster of boys.

"Yeah, I've come down specifically to watch this highly professional playground team, sure," Mae said bluntly. The boy sniggered and ran back to the game, Murmurs of 'who is she?' rang out. Sean looked over, saw Mae and waved.

Mae walked on, approaching their flimsy wooden gate. The ashen grey concrete of their low-rise home blended with the cloudy night-sky. She rustled around under the dustbin for the key and let herself in. From her kitchen, she could hear the clatter of dinner plates being placed on the drying rack next door and the mum calling the names of her two squealing kids. And after that, silence as they watched television.

Mae looked in her fridge. It contained a small wedge of cheese, two eggs and an old tin of soup. Then she rooted around the cupboards. They were empty, but for the residue of some porridge oat dust and bread crumbs. Sean would have sat down with his family for a hearty meal of sausages and mashed potato or fish and chips if his parents fancied a takeaway. But Mae was alone, her household dark and dinnerless. She walked her deflated body up the cold stairway and sank into the cocoon of her butterfly duvet with her blue-tacked shrine of female pop musicians watching over her.

In the morning, Mae quickly washed her face and armpits and dragged her uniform on. The silence in the house was unsettled by the creaks of the floorboards as she moved around. Lily wasn't up, and Nick had perhaps stayed at a friend's house. She walked herself to school.

Mae heard a voice behind calling her name and heaved a deep sigh. She tentatively turned her head and was relieved as her eyes detected strands of Imogen's fiery ginger hair.

"Good morning my little Mavis! Did you see Arsenal last night? Jordan Nobbs scored a belter! Clattering volley straight in the top corner. Unreal."

"Who are you calling Mavis? No, I missed it, I didn't really feel in the mood," Mae replied.

"You alright, Mae? It's not like you, you're usually giving me the post-match analysis!" Imogen put her hand on Mae's shoulder and tilted her freckled face with concern.

"Yeah, just Mum is being weird, she's stressed. We went to watch Nick play yesterday anyway."

"Oh yeah? The golden boy scored some goals did he?" Imogen mocked.

"Yeah, the Messi of Malvern Rovers did Lil proud, eh. I can't believe I've spent so much time watching him, an entire childhood of Sunday football in the spitting rain."

"You're a professional at watching amateur boys' football, I'd say. Get this girl a medal."

Mae laughed.

The thin silhouette of a teenage boy shuffled up alongside Mae and Imogen. His ill-fitting school suit swamped him. "Am the man, on time are we!" Imogen tossed her head back and laughed.

"Always right on time. What are we talking about?"

The three of them now walked together as a unit, slowly ambling at the

FICTION

back of the herds of kids and trying to lengthen their catch-up time.

"Imogen was just saying how I deserve a medal for going to watch my brother's football team since I was in nappies," Mae quipped.

"Why aren't you playing, though?" Amir questioned.

"I don't know, I've got too much going on," Mae said.

"Your family's stressed so you can't play?" Imogen probed.

Mae looked into the distance while turning Imogen's words around in her head. "They're not your responsibility, Mae," Imogen added.

"I know, I don't care anyway. Lily has made it very clear she doesn't care about me being able to play. She thinks football's for Nick, not me. She'd have set up her own team for him."

"Maybe she's scared that you'll get stick for playing. Nick is the textbook strong man. That makes it easy for people to picture him in a football team. People have weird ideas of what a footballer does and doesn't look like," Amir suggested.

Mae nodded.

"Is that what you want her to do, set up a girls' team?" Imogen continued.

"I mean that would be absolutely top-tier Mum behaviour, but no. She'd never do that."

"So, you'll find another way," Imogen reassured, her mane of red hair glowing against the grey sky.

Mae felt a cloud beginning to dissipate. She knew it wasn't easy for her to play football. No one was inviting her to play or telling her it was a birthright, but it didn't mean she couldn't. Nick commanded power and respect in the cliquish corner of the community they belonged to in their gossipy small town. It was a society he so easily slotted into. But no one was watching what Mae did or expecting her to score goals on repeat, get signed at one of the academies and follow through the pipeline to becoming a professional. *Why shouldn't that be expected? But maybe that lack of expectation didn't have to be such a bad thing.*

On her way home from school, Mae stopped at Nana Polly's house.

"Chook!" Polly took half of Mae's face in her soft, Nivea-scented hands.

"You've been a total stranger, you had me wondering what had happened to my Mae!"

Mae beamed, humouring Nana's usual claims of neglect. Polly had short, dusty silver hair and bright cheeks. Nana's house was a white cobbled cottage with a cobalt blue door. Framing it was lush grass, brimming with immaculate hydrangeas, lavender and foxgloves, like one of those flower show gardens.

Nana brought out the tin of fancy biscuits she reserved for these late afternoon visits and handed Mae a sugary mug of tea-infused milk. She liked after-school time spent with Nana whose walls were busily filled with colourful abstract prints, and whose face was always lit with a smile. The house was warm and bright. Mae sank deeper into the sofa and felt Nana's warm hand pat her back.

"So what's new?" Nana asked, eagerly.

"Same old really, Nana, just school, mock exams next week, nothing exciting."

"What do you think you'll do with yourself after school? Dare I mention that?" Nana asked, chuckling softly.

"I don't know, college maybe," Mae said flatly.

"Don't sound too excited! What do you really like doing? I know you're a star student, but I reckon you'd enjoy a good time every now and then too," Nana replied.

"It'd be great to play football, if that were possible, like," Mae said, as if she was thinking to herself.

"Brilliant! Well, you know that you want to play, now it's a case of working out how to make that happen."

Nana launched herself up from the sofa as Mae murmured, "try telling Mum that."

"Let me show you something, you'll love it," Nana said before Mae heard her rooting around drawers in the hallway.

When Nana reappeared, she had a small picture frame resting in her hands, and fond memories flashed over her face. She handed the frame to Mae and turned on the couch to see her reaction. Mae's eyes searched up and down. The photo was grainy in texture. Two lines of children squinted into the camera. They looked tired and had muddy faces and shirts. A football rested at the front of the frame. As she examined the picture closely, Mae noticed there were two girls in the crowd of boys.

"This was your mum, aged eight, when she played for the local boys' team," Nana summarised, in case the guessing game hadn't worked.

"What do you mean?" Mae queried.

"Your mum played from the age of eight. To around 15, it would have been."

"She never told me," Mae asserted, her voice stinging. "Actually, she told me I couldn't play. Even though she did, for all those years," she continued.

Nana placed the photo down on the sideboard and wrapped her arms around Mae.

"Listen Mae, it wasn't the easiest time for her toward the end. I'd just left her dad, we were short of money and then she'd go to football, which she'd always loved, until the coach started to tell her she was playing like a girl if she made a mistake. One day, the coach sat her down and told her she couldn't play anymore. That's not me excusing your mum, I'm just saying that she was left with very mixed feelings," Nana said softly.

"So, because it was hard for her, I have to go through the same," Mae sighed.

"I know what you're saying Mae, but I don't see why it has to be that way. Quite the opposite," Nana affirmed. Drilling down into the practicalities, she asked, "Is there a girls' team you could play for?"

"No," Mae replied.

Then she thought about the boys in the play area and reconsidered. "There must be a way though."

Mae walked home as dusk started to settle. She took the long route, down the hill, over the railway track, and across the playing field. From a distance, Mae saw outlines of two people kicking a ball between themselves. As she passed, the ball veered toward her. Mae felt a dread-filled cramp in her stomach as it advanced, knowing that it would cross her path and tangle with her feet. *Would she be able to kick it? Stop it even?* The doubts howled harshly in her mind.

Mae then stopped the ball. She felt a rush of joy as her foot connected with it. She lunged forward and returned the ball back to a smiling girl who stood a few metres apart from a grown-up man—her dad, Mae supposed.

Mae wanted her Dad to take her to the playing field and kick a ball in the cold muddiness. But her family, as Mae had known it, had shattered into sharp pieces like a beer bottle clumsily dropped. She remembered Rick crying along to Lily's yells. He was long and thin like a tower, but in the end he seemed so small. Mae wanted to pick him up like the tiny shards of spiky glass that were at his feet when he dropped the bottle for the last time. She wanted to hold him.

Lily cleared up the broken glass quickly. First, she shouted, then there was silence as she swept the remnants away before manically hoovering every last shard. Eventually, Rick went too. The second last text Mae had got from Rick said "hey wavy Maevy, how are you kid? Dad XXX", before the final one just a few hours later in the early hours of the morning: "hiy kidd. Im sory, i lov u." He left bereft cupboards, cold darkness that haunted every corner of the house, and quiet sadness in his wake.

***

Lily walked up the hill. Cars flew past on the road beside her, a sea of shiny SUVs on lease deals. The bus had been late again, she'd waited 15 minutes and given up. The food bank would close at seven, and she'd need to beat the queues or else she'd be there deep into the evening. There would usually be more people standing in line there than for a Boxing Day sale. People shifted their weight from one foot to the other in the queue. It was cold, but it's also what the stress and unshakeable fear of waking up the next day and having nothing to eat did to people.

Lily quickened her pace, always rushing and pushing forward, but she felt like she was going backwards. She thought of how Mae wanted to play football. She could see it in how Mae watched the boys play with wonder glittering her eyes. Lily's chest was heavy with guilt. She'd told her she couldn't play. Lily had thought she'd be the mother who championed her daughter playing football, who fought against every obstacle. But in reality, she'd run out of steam. *Her instinct to protect Mae was stifling her daughter's hopes*, Lily thought. She knew what it was like to feel joy on the pitch, to have the ball at your feet, to look up and toward the goal with a smile on your face in the dappled light. She knew the magic of playing. Things were harder now, though. Rick couldn't contribute any money and she was trying to keep her family above water in a low-paid job without any contracted hours. That felt like enough of a struggle.

Lily recalled being lumped on the bench at age 15 during the last match of the season. Phil, the bullish coach, walked over to her. He stopped at her feet, looming with his arms folded and puffing up his sleeping bag jacket before lifting one of his Nike trainers so it straddled the seat. Phil was one of the boy's dads—no certificate or talent qualified him as a coach, more just an innate brutishness which he felt made him up to the job. He opened his mouth and drawled as if the conversation were an inconvenience.

"Doll you're not a bad player and that, but as we move up the league and the standards get high, it'll just be for the lads now, I'm afraid." He sucked the snot from his sinuses, projecting his thick yellow spit onto the white sideline. As if her fate wasn't already clear, he sealed it with another not-so-accidental affront.

"So this will be your last game, love. Make it count." Lily peeled off into the boys' changing room, locked herself in the toilet and let the tears silently fall.

***

Mae walked quickly down the hill, taking a left toward the play area. The boys were there. She walked through the gate and beyond the threshold of the railings. Her heart was racing but she kept walking toward the group. "I'm in," Mae announced loudly. The boys' heads turned in unison, their darting eyes running over her. It seemed like half a minute of silence ensued.

"Ha, you're joking," one boy said gruffly.

"Yeah, as if you're playing with us," another chimed in.

Mae challenged, "I don't care, I'll play against you. I'll beat you too."

The high-pitched laughs grew louder and lasted longer.

"Get out, we're playing football here," the small boy with the missing tooth said. His friends laughed some more.

Sean rubbed his face and looked down at the ground.

"You heard him, go away you lesbian," said the tall boy, chortling.

"Have you got a problem with lesbians, is that what this is?" Mae asked angrily.

"Hey! Lads, why are you saying that? …It's not our park, she has a right to be here too," Sean said tentatively at first, but finished off more certain of what he was saying.

"Fine, forget it. You can stay," conceded the tall boy.

"By the way, I don't know what made you think it'd be funny, but being a lesbian isn't an insult so don't try that again," Mae challenged.

If Mae was going to start playing football, she needed to set off on the right foot. The boy who had looked so tall and formidable when she watched him the other day was now red-faced and looked small. He somehow forced out a "sorry" and they started to play. As Mae dribbled the ball, she couldn't believe how long it had taken her to cross the sideline, but now she was

FICTION

there, she couldn't see herself going back.

Mae marched into the changing room, jittery in her determination. She delved into her kit bag for her silky shirt and shorts. She pulled the kit on, took a deep breath and looked at herself in the mirror. Mae was honouring the young girl who wanted to play. The one whose story had started all those years ago in the play area around the corner from her estate.

Olivia Barber is a writer and aspiring journalist who plays football at a grassroots level in the UK. Her blog, Halftime Oranges, highlights hidden stories from women's football culture in the UK and other parts of Europe.

Izzy's Magical Soccer Adventure

by Emma Larkin

Chapter 1

It was a frosty Sunday morning in February. The sun was shining, but it was so cold I could see my breath moving in the air. I kept blowing out of my mouth so that I could see the shapes it made; it looked really cool.

I was out in my backyard doing keepie-uppies with a ball. We often had fun competitions at soccer training to see who could do the most, so I was practising. I wanted to be in with a chance of winning at training.

"Izzy!" Mum's voice distracted me, and I dropped the ball.

"Aaah Mum, I nearly got to 20 keepie-uppies!" I whined.

"Izzy, put on your hat, it's really cold."

Mum was waving my hat at me from the back door.

"Mum, you made me drop the ball," I moaned.

"Oops, sorry love," Mum replied. "It's just that it's freezing cold and I don't want you to get sick."

"OK Mum," I grumbled. "I've loads of clothes on, but I suppose a hat would help."

It **was** *really* cold. Also, it was a cool bobble hat in Bally FC's colours of green and yellow.

I had been playing soccer with Bally FC since January and I absolutely loved it. My best friend Cara played as well. We were both in the U-10 team. Her dad, Pat, was one of our coaches. We trained every Sunday morning.

I still enjoyed playing Gaelic football and camogie, but Bally GAA (the Gaelic football club) wouldn't start training again until March or April. Right now, soccer training and matches with Bally FC were keeping me

FICTION

busy—which was fine with me.

"Izzy, will you play with Boots for a while?" Dad asked, walking toward me.

He was just back from a walk with Boots, our puppy. She's six months old and is already a big dog, full of energy!

"OK, Dad," I grinned.

Boots is great for practising soccer with until she starts trying to eat the ball! When I play in the garden, Boots is like the best defender in the world. She never stops trying to get the ball from me.

Scoring goals is my favourite thing to do in soccer matches. At U-10 soccer training, we still move around and try out different positions on the pitch, but Cara and I are fairly sure that we have found our natural homes—her as a defender and me as a striker.

"I thought you might like some practise with Boots," Dad laughed. "Just don't tire yourself out too much before training."

"I won't, Dad," I replied, "Can you take my bracelet inside?" I asked, unclasping it from my wrist. "I'm afraid Boots will break it!"

"No problem, Izzy," Dad smiled, "we all know how special this bracelet is to you."

"Thanks Dad," I grinned.

If he only knew! My bracelet is no ordinary bracelet. My great-grandmother won three All-Ireland medals playing for her county and a jeweller made the medals into a bracelet for her. She gave it to my Mum who passed it on to me.

I absolutely adore it. Amazingly, the bracelet has taken me on three magical journeys in my imagination—first to Croke Park in the future where I played in a ladies' Gaelic football match for my county. Then, last summer, it took me to Croke Park in the past, where I saw my great-grandmother playing a camogie match. My third magical adventure was just two months ago at Christmas when it took Boots and me to the North Pole.

These magical adventures were always a surprise but so much fun.

"Woof, woof!!"

Boots was jumping up and down with excitement. She really wanted to play with my ball. Boots would run all day long—she never seemed to tire out.

I started racing around the garden, dribbling the ball at my feet, swerving as fast as I could to try and avoid Boots. My brothers, Robert, Patrick and David soon arrived outside, having heard her happy barks.

We ended up playing a quick 2 v 2 game of soccer. Patrick and me against David and Robert, our usual teams. My big brother, David, the eldest in the family, with Robert, the youngest, and then Patrick with me. It was the fairest way to split the teams.

Boots was running around like an extra defender for whichever team didn't have the ball. We had been playing for about 10 minutes when I heard a car horn beeping. The score was 2-2. I didn't want to leave. as we were really close to scoring a third goal. We had sent a few balls wide, but I could feel that a goal was coming.

"Izzy, that's Pat here to collect you for training," Patrick said. "Don't worry, I'll go on and win the game for us. Boots will help me," he grinned.

"I think this match is ours," David laughed.

"Have fun at training, we'll miss you," Robert shouted as he kicked the ball out of the goal area.

"You won't miss me Robert," I shouted back, sticking out my tongue at him. "You're happy I'm leaving because I was so close to scoring a goal!"

"In your dreams, Izzy," was the last thing I heard Robert say as I ran toward Pat's car.

Chapter 2

I climbed into the back seat of Pat's car panting after the game with the boys.

"What's up, Izzy?" Cara smiled at me.

She didn't really expect an answer. That was just our usual way of saying hello to each other.

I grinned back at her.

"Nothing much, what's up with you?"

She was wearing the same green and yellow bobble hat as me, and the rest of the Bally FC kit. Our jersey was lovely. It was green with a diagonal yellow stripe down the front. The shorts were green with yellow stripes on the sides and our socks were green with yellow stripes around the top.

"Have you got your shin guards on, Izzy?" Pat asked.

"I sure do," I laughed. "Remember the time when I forgot them, Cara, and I got a kick in the shin? I had a huge bruise for weeks afterwards."

"Ugh, I remember," Cara shuddered. "That looked so sore."

"You see," Pat added, "shin guards are very important for soccer."

"We know, Dad," Cara rolled her eyes, and we grinned at each other.

"You seem a bit out of breath, Izzy," Pat said.

"I was playing soccer with my brothers and Boots just now in the garden," I replied.

"Oh Boots is such a good defender!" Cara squealed.

"Yeah, but she has burst so many balls," I groaned. "She is just too enthusiastic trying to get it."

Pat laughed as we drove into the Bally FC grounds.

"What a lovely morning for soccer," he said, parking the car.

We quickly hopped out and ran over to our teammates. Some of the girls went to different schools, but we had all become great friends.

The hour of training passed quickly. We had so much fun. We warmed-up first, then we practised our dribbling. Next, we did our keepie-uppie competition. I came second after Cara. She got 25 in a row, I got 23. Finally, we had a practice match. The girls said I was on fire! I scored three goals and our team won 3–1.

"You were flying it today, Izzy," Cara said as we walked back to the car after training. "You were on target so many times and scored three goals."

"I love being a striker and scoring goals! You were amazing as well, Cara," I replied. "You are an absolute defensive rock."

Cara laughed. "I think my favourite place on the pitch will always be as a defender," she smiled.

Cara did more than just defend and clear the ball. She had such good vision on the pitch and started so many plays from the back—she was brilliant.

"Izzy," Pat called after me. "Can I have a word before we go home?"

I walked over to where Pat and another coach were standing.

"Izzy, this is Anne. She's a coach with the U-12 girls' soccer team here at Bally FC," Pat explained.

"Hi Izzy," Anne smiled at me.

"Um, hi," I replied, not sure what was going on.

"Izzy," Anne smiled, "the U-12 team have a match next weekend and our striker, Grace, has broken her arm, so she can't play."

"Oh no, poor Grace," I said sadly.

"She will make a full recovery," Anne said. "But we have a problem for our match next weekend. It's a semi-final against Grange FC and we have no striker. We were wondering if you would play for us?"

"Me?" I asked in amazement.

"Yes, you," Anne grinned. "I've watched you play and you are a natural goal scorer. We could do with your help. Will you play with us?"

Pat gave me a proud grin.

"It's fine with your mum and dad, Izzy. I checked." Pat said. "If you want to play, that is?"

"Wow, I would love to," I beamed. "Thanks so much for asking me!"

"Great," Anne said. "That's settled. It's a home match here next Saturday. See you then, Izzy."

FICTION

Chapter 3

When I got home after training, Mum and Dad were delighted to hear that I was going to be playing with the U-12s.

Even Patrick was impressed. I could tell, even though he would never admit it.

I was so excited about the U-12 match. I practised every day out in the garden that week. I worked on penalties as well—just in case. Robert is a whiz as a goalie, so I asked him to stand in goals and I practised taking shots on him.

When Saturday rolled around, I was ready. My kit, boots and shin guards were laid out from the night before. I got up, quickly dressed and headed downstairs for breakfast. I left my magic bracelet safely on my bedside table as jewellery is not allowed to be worn during a match.

Mum, Dad and my three brothers came with me to the match. I felt very calm as I headed onto the pitch. I didn't know many of the U-12 girls, but they all waved and smiled at me, as did Anne, the coach.

"Girls, this is Izzy," Anne said. "She is playing up front for us today, as Grace is still off injured.

"Hi Izzy," the girls all said together.

"Great to have you playing, Izzy," a tall girl said loudly. "I'm Olivia, the captain today,"

"Izzy loves scoring goals so let's get that ball to her. Just watch the play, Izzy, and make sure you aren't offside," Anne smiled.

"OK," I nodded.

David had explained the offside rule to me a few weeks before and I was certain that I knew what to do. He said that it was a rule to make sure that a player on one team, usually a striker, can't just hang around really close to the goal waiting to score. The offside rule means that a player is offside if they get the ball while being beyond the second-last opponent, who is usually a defender.

The match started off in a cagey fashion. Both teams knew that a place in the final was up for grabs, and nobody wanted to risk making a mistake.

Finally, with only two minutes left to play in the first half, one of our midfielders, Emily, made a spectacular burst through opposing players and delivered a perfect pass to me. I controlled the ball by stopping it dead with my foot. Like lightning, I took the ball around the last defender and boom, into the back of the net!

I punched the air—my first goal for the U-12s!

We were still leading 1-0 at halftime. The girls all patted me on the back as we caught our breath at the break. We quickly grabbed our bottles and took a gulp of water. We were dying with thirst from all the running.

"Great teamwork," Anne told us. "Keep it up girls. Stay very alert in defence. They will be working hard to draw level."

Sure enough, despite heroic efforts by the Bally defenders, Grange FC managed to score from a corner not long after the restart. Our girls were tiring, and after another 10 minutes, we let in another goal. I groaned. Now Grange was winning 2-1.

Right, I thought, we don't have long left, we need an equaliser.

I kept working hard, watching the play in midfield, making runs and trying to get myself in a good position. Finally, with three minutes left on the clock, it paid off. I managed to win the ball at the side of the pitch.

I took off up the sideline, swerving past a Grange player. I was heading straight for the goal.

I looked up. There was one more defender ahead of me. I made a move as if to try and pass her on the right, but instead darted to the left. She was caught off guard, going right and then quickly trying to move back to the left. As I was about to get past her, she stuck her leg out. I felt a stab of pain as her boot connected with my shin and I fell to the ground.

"Penalty, penalty!"

I could hear shouts from all around me as I slowly stood up. I bent down and gingerly felt my leg. It was a little sore to touch, but nothing too bad. I knew I could play on.

"Are you OK, Izzy?" Emily asked.

"Yes, it's just a bruise I think," I replied.

I looked at the referee and she was pointing to the penalty spot.

"Are you sure you are OK to take it, Izzy?" Anne shouted from the sideline. "Is your leg alright?"

"It's fine," I nodded.

"You've got this, Izzy," smiled Olivia, our captain, patting me on the back.

I took a deep breath and looked at the goalie. She was so tall. I suddenly felt goosebumps on my arms. I was nervous. I had practised taking penalties at home on Robert, but this was so different. Everyone was looking at me.

"Come on Izzy," I muttered to myself.

I took a run-up to the ball, thinking that I would go to the right. But at the last minute, I changed my mind in a panic and decided to shoot to the left.

Bang.

I watched in horror as my shot sailed wide and the Grange players all punched the air.

A minute later, they were running around hugging each other, delighted with their win. I was so upset that I had missed the chance to level the match. I had cost our team a place in the final.

"Hard luck, girls," Anne said with a sympathetic look as we trudged to the dugout. "It was just one of those days. You all worked very hard."

"Pity about that shot going wide, Izzy," Emily said as we sat down to take off our boots.

I wasn't sure if she was being mean. She didn't sound it, but I couldn't be sure.

"Did you change your mind about the direction you were going to shoot?" Olivia asked.

"I did," I said, surprised. "How did you know?"

"First rule of penalties," Olivia said seriously. "Never change your mind."

"Oh, I didn't know that, sorry," I mumbled, close to tears.

"Don't worry, it happens to all of us," Olivia smiled as she walked away.

I was miserable as I climbed into the car to go home.

"Don't worry Izzy," Mum said to me with a smile. "The best players miss penalties. You scored a lovely goal today; you should be very proud of yourself."

But I couldn't get excited about the fact that I'd scored a goal for the U-12s. The penalty miss was all I could think about.

"I'm never taking a penalty again, Mum," I vowed.

Patrick looked at me. I could tell he was about to say something mean but then he changed his mind. He must have seen the tear falling slowly down my cheek.

I sat in silence all the way home.

Chapter 4

Luckily, I had something to take my mind off the penalty miss and losing the semi-final. The following week Bally FC were taking all the underage players to watch the Ireland women's soccer team play against France at Tallaght Stadium in Dublin. It was a group match in the World Cup Qualifiers. If Ireland won, we were guaranteed a spot at the World Cup.

The big day finally arrived. I carefully fixed my magic bracelet onto my wrist. *It might bring Ireland luck today*, I thought.

"This is such a huge match for Ireland," Cara shouted excitedly.

We were waiting at the Bally FC clubhouse for the bus to take us to Dublin. There was a big group of us and we were all a bit 'hyper'.

"I know," I replied to Cara. "I hope they can win it and then we'll be in the World Cup, imagine that!"

"Are you still sad about missing the penalty in the match?" Cara asked.

"A bit," I said slowly. "Look the bus is here, race you to the back seats!"

FICTION

We ran up the steps onto the bus. All the girls were singing *Olé, Olé, Olé* as Cara and I plopped down into our seats. We joined in, singing as loudly as we could.

The three-hour trip to Dublin passed quickly. We were all singing and playing games. *Olé, Olé, Olé* was stuck in my brain as we arrived at Tallaght Stadium.

"This is going to be a tough match," Cara said as we got off the bus. "France is really good."

"Imagine if we qualify for the World Cup!" Maeve, one of our teammates, shouted excitedly.

"Ireland has a great chance," I grinned. "Our girls are improving all the time and playing really well."

"I can't wait for this," Cara said, beaming.

Both the noise and the atmosphere inside Tallaght Stadium were unbelievable. The stadium was full and everyone was singing. And the match hadn't even started.

"Oh, thank you," we all shouted. The coaches had given us all yummy bags of chips. It was fantastic watching the teams warming up on the pitch and eating those tasty chips!

"This is brilliant," I said, munching happily. "But how come Ireland's women's team doesn't get to play at Aviva Stadium where the men's team play?"

"Good question, Izzy," Pat replied. "I suppose because the women's soccer team hasn't been around for as long as the men's team, so they don't get as much support. But the support is growing all the time," he added. "Look around you. I bet in a few years all these people and many more besides will be inside Aviva Stadium watching the women play and making an even louder noise!"

"I hope so," I replied.

"They should be able to play in the same stadium as the men," Cara grimaced.

"I agree completely girls," Pat smiled, nodding his head. "Look, the match is starting now. Come on everyone, get up and cheer on our team."

The match was so exciting. Only five minutes after kick-off, Ireland scored! The crowd went wild. We were all cheering and hugging.

"I can't believe Ireland got an early goal!" I said to Cara.

"I know," Cara replied. "It's so cool! France has so many superstar players, everyone thought they were going to win!"

"Well there's loads of time to play yet," I added. "But it's great to have scored a goal against them."

"Yup," Cara nodded. "Our girls really came out all guns blazing, didn't they?"

I nodded in agreement.

It was still 1-0 to Ireland at halftime, although France had by far the most chances at goal. Our defenders and goalie had played especially well. Ireland had pulled everyone back after the early goal.

"I hope they can keep it going in the second half," Cara muttered in my ear. The noise was so loud, I could barely hear her.

"I hope so too," I said nervously, my mind going back to the U-12 match against Grange the week before. It all felt so similar.

I checked that my bracelet was on my wrist and stood up to wave my Ireland flag as the teams ran out onto the pitch for the second half.

The French team attacked furiously. The Irish players tried everything to block them, but after 15 tense minutes, a French striker broke through and scored.

The small number of French supporters in the crowd went wild. They shouted and waved flags. The Irish crowd stayed silent.

"Oh no," Cara groaned.

"Don't worry, Cara," I said, more confidently than I felt. "Our girls won't let their heads drop."

I was right. Ireland responded really well. They attacked straight away

FICTION

and 10 minutes after the French goal, an Irish player was brought down in the box.

All the Bally FC girls started shouting "penalty, penalty!". Suddenly, it seemed like the whole stadium had joined in with our chant and were shouting "penalty!".

I looked down and the referee was indeed pointing to the spot. Penalty! The noise in the stadium grew even louder and all you could see were Irish flags waving.

"Why are you so quiet, Izzy?" Cara asked, as she danced around yelling and waving her flag. "We have a penalty. Stephanie Murphy, our captain, is going to take it."

"I know," I said. "But what if she misses, like I did last weekend? I feel so nervous for her, I can't watch."

"Oh Izzy," Cara said. "This is a totally different game. Come here, hold my hand," she reassured as the Irish captain stepped up to take the shot.

I held onto Cara tightly and rubbed my bracelet with my other hand to try and bring Stephanie some luck. I felt so scared for her. I looked up slowly as she began her run-up to kick the ball. But then, suddenly, my great-grandmother's bracelet started to feel hot on my wrist. The familiar swirling and spinning sensation started.

"Izzy," Cara said, looking worried, "something strange is happening. I think I'm going to faint."

I realised that I was still holding onto Cara.

"You're not going to faint, Cara," I smiled, feeling calm for the first time in weeks. "I think we're going on a magic adventure!"

"What!" Cara shouted as the bright lights flashed and we were sucked into a black tunnel.

I was going on another magical adventure and Cara was coming with me. I couldn't believe it!

Chapter 5

"Izzy," Cara whispered nervously as the tunnel came to an end.

Both of us started blinking furiously as the bright sunlight hit our eyes.

"Izzy," Cara repeated. "Where are we?"

I looked around as my eyes adjusted to the light. We were on a soccer pitch in a huge, modern stadium. It was full of people waving Irish flags and cheering. I looked down. I was wearing an Ireland soccer kit with my shin guards on. I was standing on perfectly green, short grass.

I could see huge green flags waving everywhere in the massive crowd and the noise was unbelievable.

"No way!" I muttered. "Has the magic bracelet taken me to Aviva Stadium? The home of Irish soccer!"

Oh wow! Magic bracelet, you have really outdone yourself this time – this is AMAZING!

But wait, I wondered, am I a grown-up again like in my first magic adventure? I looked at my legs and arms and realised that I was.

But where was Cara? She had disappeared.

"Izzy," I heard my name and turned around. It was Cara, or at least I thought it was. She was dressed in the same kit as me, an Ireland soccer kit. She was standing exactly where I would expect her to be on the pitch: the centre-back position. She gave a small wave and smiled at me. She looked nervous, but maybe a little excited. I was standing just ahead of the halfway line.

"IZZY!" I heard a roar from a voice that definitely wasn't Cara. "Pay attention Izzy," the voice from the sideline shouted. "What's wrong with you, the ball is in play?"

It must be our coach. Wow, I really did seem to be on the Irish senior women's soccer team. What an amazing magical adventure.

I realised that the coach was shouting at me because the ball had been kicked out by the other team's goalie. I was miles away from where I should be on the pitch. *Run Izzy!* I thought as I gritted my teeth. *Who are we playing?* I also wondered.

A stop in play for an injury on the other side of the pitch gave me the minute I needed to run down to Cara.

"Cara," I hissed in her ear, "We're on a magical adventure!"

"I know," Cara whispered back. "You shouldn't be down here, Izzy. I'm a centre-back, you should be up front."

I grinned. "Just like when we play with Bally FC. Do you know who we're playing Cara?"

Cara always knew the colour of the jersey that each country wore.

"Sweden," she said firmly.

My eyes grew wide.

"They are really good," I whispered.

"Yeah, but look, it's nil-all and there's 15 minutes left to play. We have time to win this. Now go!" Cara ordered.

I ran back to my position as a striker and watched as one of our players limped off the pitch, assisted by the team doctor. That was the injury on the other side of the pitch. It dawned on me that the player going off was our other striker. Her replacement ran past me in a blur of green, patting me on the back as she went.

"Coach says good job so far, Izzy," she said, grinning. "She also said stop dreaming and put the ball in the back of the net!"

"That's what I'll do," I laughed.

This could be fun, I thought. I was going to make the most of this magical adventure. The crowd roared as the game restarted. Our players were attacking furiously. I watched in awe as Cara started so many plays from the back of the pitch like she had been doing it all her life. She was amazing. All the players were. They kept getting the ball up to me and the replacement striker, Katy.

We had linked up a few times. I had crossed into her but she missed a header. Then I very nearly scored but the Swedish goalie made a spectacular save.

I also took a free kick from outside the box and nearly looped it into the top right corner of the goal, but again their goalie stretched to her full height and saved it.

We were doing everything to score, but the Swedish defence was excellent. I was sure it was going to end in a nil-all draw. Then a minute into injury time, I passed to Katy who ran at speed toward the goals. The Swedish left back was caught off guard and made a badly-timed tackle.

I watched in slow motion as Katy fell to the ground in the box. The referee pointed to the spot: penalty! I felt that all too familiar feeling of dread in the pit of my stomach as the crowd went wild.

I couldn't believe it. Why were all these penalties happening when I was around! I hate penalties. One of our players was walking toward me. I zeroed in on the captain's armband on her arm.

"Izzy, you're up," she said, "Go get 'em."

"What?" I stuttered. "Can't Katy take it?"

She looked at me with a puzzled frown on her face.

"Izzy, you always take the penalties," she said slowly. "What's wrong with you?"

"I do?" I asked.

Cara had arrived and was nodding furiously at me.

"Yes, you do," she said firmly.

"You can do this, Izzy. You have the best attitude of any striker when it comes to penalties," our captain continued.

"Even when I miss?" I asked.

"Yes, especially when you miss. You always say that everyone misses sometimes but you never shy away from taking one. You always tell us that you should never change your mind about what side you are going to shoot to. Are you sure you're feeling alright?"

"She's fine," Cara said quickly.

"Am I?" I asked her.

Cara nodded.

I suddenly felt more positive. I am alright. I can do this. I am playing for Ireland. Any girl would love this chance. I am doing this. I am doing this!!!

I stepped up and put the ball on the spot. I turned it once for some reason. *This must be something that grown-up Izzy does,* I thought with a grin. I stepped back for my run-up. It all felt so natural. *I must do this all the time.*

It's just like in training Izzy, a voice in my head said. *Block out the noise. Don't change your mind about which way you are going to shoot.*

I closed my eyes and took a deep breath. Then I opened them. I was focused.

I ran and shot with huge power. Right-hand side, BOOM!

The keeper stood no chance.

GOALLLLL!!!

The noise came back with a bang. The crowd was standing and cheering. Everyone was waving Ireland flags with all their might.

I stood in shock as my team surrounded me, hugging me and jumping on me.

"Our record goal scorer does it again, Amy!" Katy, the other striker, shouted to our captain.

A chant rang out from around the stadium. "Izzy, Izzy, Izzy!"

"This is just the best magical adventure ever," I whispered to Cara who was standing beside me.

Cara was beaming.

"It sure is Izzy," she replied. "This is the best day of my life."

Two minutes later, the referee blew the final whistle. The match was all over. We had won 1–0 against Sweden!

"We're heading for the World Cup again girls!" Amy roared as we all hugged.

"Again?" Cara said.

Amy looked at her strangely. Cara winked at me. We both knew that in our time, Ireland had never qualified for the World Cup. This was brilliant news!

Suddenly, the all too familiar swirling started.

"We're going back, Cara," I said, grabbing my best friend's hand.

"Oh Izzy, I'm scared," she said.

"Don't be," I smiled as the black tunnel appeared. "It will all be fine."

We held hands as we were sucked into the tunnel with the lights swirling around us.

Seconds later, we were back in our seats inside Tallaght Stadium. Amazingly, no time had passed at all. Stephanie was ready to take her penalty.

"Are you OK girls?" Pat asked us. "You're sweating and you look like you've been running around."

"We're fine, Dad," Cara laughed. "We're just nervous about the penalty."

She winked at me when her dad looked away.

I wasn't nervous about the penalty anymore. I looked on in delight as Stephanie, the Irish captain and striker, hit the ball into the right-hand side of the net—just like me!

Goal for Ireland!

A nervous 15 minutes followed, but Ireland held onto the lead and won. It was their first win against France, and it meant that Ireland had qualified for the World Cup for the first time ever!

We all stayed in our seats long after the final whistle, waving our flags, cheering the players and singing songs. We even got our Ireland jerseys signed by Stephanie Murphy. It was the best night ever.

"Well girls," Pat said, as we all headed back to the bus, "you all just got to watch history in the making. The Ireland women's team is going to their first ever World Cup!"

"The first of many!" Cara shouted.

"Here's hoping," her dad replied.

I smiled at Cara behind his back.

FICTION

"Just you wait, Pat," I grinned. "Someday, you might be watching Cara and me out there playing for Ireland."

"I wouldn't doubt it for a second," Pat laughed.

I turned and high-fived Cara. We laughed as the magic bracelet made a little tinkling noise as our hands met.

The future was definitely bright and magical!

Emma Larkin is the author of unique Irish sporting-themed children's books – 'Izzy's Magical Adventures in Sport' series. She is a mother of four children and coaches the football team of one of her daughters. After this fictional story was written, Ireland did indeed qualify for their first ever Women's World Cup when they beat Scotland in front of 10,000 fans in Glasgow to secure their place for the 2023 event in Australia and New Zealand. They are in the group stage with home team Australia, Canada and Nigeria.

Personal Stories

My Love is for the Red, Red Rose

by Amy Canavan

I fell head over heels in love with the Scottish Professional Football League's (SPFL's) newest club, Bonnyrigg Rose, with help from Sean Connery, East Kilbride, and the great-grandfather I never knew.

Monster truck tyres. Stock car racing track. Meshed safety fence. Main stand divided in two. Half wooden grandstand, half newly seated. Home of 'The Blue Brazil'. The 'Fife Maracanã'.

The outlandish scene of Central Park–Cowdenbeath Football Club's ground–has long been woven into the rich tapestry of Scottish football as one of the great, outrageous arenas to inhale a game of 'shooty-in'.

On Saturday, 14 May 2022, it facilitated an overwhelming, landmark moment in Bonnyrigg Rose's 141-year-long history.

Since the old league structure disintegrated—despite some ploughing on with redundant terminology for more than a decade—and the SPFL emerged, three teams have inflicted the Scottish footballing equivalent of a public execution.

The audacity of the pyramid system play-offs to offer an opportunity for tier five teams to wrestle with the status quo of the failing teams annually propping up the foot of tier four, had many sniffing blood. Noses in and around the county eight miles south-east of Edinburgh enlarged.

For as far back as the history books go, the senior Scottish leagues were notoriously a shut-up-shop. Blink, and you'll have missed the once-in-a-blue moon window of sneaking in due to a club liquidation, league reconstruction or a good old-fashioned vote.

In 2013, when the SPFL was born and the pyramid play-off system had aspiring, predominantly former-junior sides rubbing their hands together, I was a mere bairn. Indulging in my beloved Celtic triumphing against the greatest team of all time, the tika-taka extraordinaries–Pep Guardiola's Barcelona. Little did I know that in a matter of years I'd be unequivocally opting for the Rosey Posey (Bonnyrigg Rose) title party, rather than the Hoops.

The word 'opting' is selling it short, considerably. Perhaps not at the forefront, but certainly closest behind the camera, gripping the microphone tightly, I uttered the words of Bonnyrigg Rose's promotion to the professional game. The big leagues. My 'Andres Cantor calling Argentina's World Cup victory' moment. Enunciating the final nails in Cowdenbeath's coffin after a 117-year stay.

A stay as long as my family's ties with the Rose.

Where the blossoming began

Few achievements can be agreed upon in Scottish football. And even then, assuming agreement produces unity would be foolish. One happened on Thursday, 25 May 1967 when 'The Lisbon Lions' (Celtic) roared. They brought the 'Big Cup' (the European Cup) to wee Scotland where it hit British shores for the first time. It was the single greatest accomplishment of any team from the land.

One year prior though, to the day, a far more amorous success sent joy up and down the east coast of the country. Well, in Midlothian, at least. But given the scorn split down the middle of the map for what goes on either side, you can guarantee a fair few more smiles were shared for the Rose's capture of 'The Holy Grail'.

Junior football is the soul of the game. It was far from the flavour and finesse dually deployed by the late, great Pelé in the heart-breaking 1966 World Cup weeks later south of the border, but it was synonymous in fervour and fight.

Forced into a replay on a wet and windy Wednesday night at the national stadium, Rose ran rampant, inflicting a 6–1 thumping against Whitburn in the Scottish Junior Cup final.

For the first time, in front of a 10,000-strong replay crowd—20,000 at the initial final—the red and white stripes lifted the special silverware. As the open-top bus attracted thousands to the streets of Boomtown and the players lapped up the adulation on their return, a slightly older man felt like a youth again as he immersed himself in the celebrations. He was such a vital cog in its creation.

John Allan. Chairman of Bonnyrigg Rose. My great-grandfather. He combusted with pride as his team ventured up the street where he was born, passing by his childhood home, which became his children's home and then his grandchildren's home. There was a little light on with the curtains drawn in the corner house, and my then 28-day-old Dad cradled by my grandmother near the window to catch a glimpse of the jubilations. Of course, my old man remembers it as clear as day...

Thankfully for him though, the family affiliation and memories with the club didn't stop there. It was a team effort on the pitch, matched by one off it. As is so often the case at the local level, it truly was a family affair. My great-grandmother sacrificed more than most, though. I imagine she'd be envious of those who only had to wash the strips and make the tea. For her, she gave up her home.

As 'head honcho', John Allan dutifully opened his—and his family's—doors to Rose players who needed a bed for a night or so around training and game schedules. Many men waltzed in and out of the revolving door of 2 Park Crescent, including a bright-eyed, bushy-eyebrowed Sean Connery.

007. Bond, James Bond. If only they had known what he was to later become, I might not even be telling this tale, and instead be swanning around in Los Angeles or somewhere exotic with even just a slithering cut of his fortunes.

Before slipping into the mould of the secret agent though, Connery snuck in and out of the Rose team in 1951, picking up pockets on the outside-right and pinging a 30-yard screamer past Broxburn Athletic.

Alas, the story with one of Scotland's most famous sons ends with a "thank you" note tucked away in my auntie's big box labelled "old stuff"… an absolute cheek to chuck Sir Sean in with 'stuff'.

While Mr "shaken, not stirred" skirted out of postcode EH19, leaving it far behind in his rear-view mirror, clan Allan, turned Canavan (my eventual family), lingered. While the role of chairman was never quite replicated, many a grandson of Allan sensed the same importance in their role as ball boys—for who else is going to force a cheer from the crowd when they petulantly fling the round leather thing in the opposing direction of the miffed rival?

You'd be forgiven for thinking that anecdotes involving *People's* "Sexiest Man of the Century" living in the same dwelling as the one I devoured Giant Strawb sweeties in would be the main tale around every dinner table. However, you'd be wrong.

For some time, my Dad has put his own spin on the veracious saying, "nowt stranger than folk," changing the latter to family. Never a truer word has left that man's mouth, unless he is declaring that I am his favourite child, of course; also a rarity.

Despite our lives being dictated by sport, primarily football, the tales I've just told were not entwined in my upbringing. However, his inch-perfect—undoubtedly illegal—sliding challenge that brought a halt to

Dalkeith Thistle's forward in 1987 has been recited so many times, I feel as though I was there.

Sure, I knew my Dad was a ball boy and a player for the then-associated amateur team, as well as an avid fan, but I was oblivious to the deep-rooted connections my family had with the Bonnyrigg club. My grandmother passed when I was just three, leaving only my Dad to foghorn the stories as his relationship with his brothers faded. Not a peep from him.

So, when the position as volunteer media officer at Bonnyrigg Rose was advertised, I saw it as nothing more than working for a local club with whom I'd taken in a few games.

Being tagged a 'glory hunter' is nothing new for one from the east coast supporting Celtic. Cries of "why don't you just support Hearts or Hibs?" (the 'big' teams from the capital) were routinely thrown in my direction. But I absolutely was a glory hunter when it came to turning up at Rose games with my Dad. League title-winning days, Scottish Cup dates and local derbies were all I kitted out for. To suggest I was besotted by the charming name before I became the club's media officer would be a far cry from reality.

But what I was on the cusp of signing up for included everything from The Rock to Raydale. Numbness at Netherdale to scenes at Shielfield. Catastrophe at Christie Gillies Park to celebrations at Calderwood. A true love affair. Buckle up for a seat on the 'Boomtown bus'… which often departed at unearthly hours of Saturday mornings… to tour the land.

Returning to the roots

For the first few months of the role though, a bus could only be dreamt of. It was the time of the coronavirus pandemic. A time in which no one knew when, where or how normality was going to return. Yet in a funny way, that was like the job description for my role in the Rose's newly formed media team—bringing football back to the people.

PERSONAL STORIES

Turnstiles locked. Gates slammed shut. Stands stood eerily quiet and still. The essence of football sucked out of the game in one, foul slurp. Alongside two other budding journalism students, we were tasked with dishing up a serving to fans from afar.

Presented with a blank canvas, we just had to bring the paintbrushes and palette to create something not even close to resembling a masterpiece. Doused in live streams and podcasts, we were pummelling the Twitter timeline with anything and everything we could conjure up. Artistic licence may daunt some, but that was not where my hesitance or worry headed; it was in relation to connection and affiliation.

While my Dad may call Bonnyrigg home, I now do not. There are three-and-a-half miles between his childhood home and our humble abode in the neighbouring town of Dalkeith. Close enough that a few of us have stumbled back there from a night out, but far enough for my Mum to have her wish that neither my brother nor I have any attachment to the borough.

There is absolutely nothing wrong with Bonnyrigg, mind you. She, as wife and mother, just wanted it her way. For her offspring to be natives of her hometown. It was an unnecessary, unsubstantial but nonetheless humorous gag that ran throughout my childhood and up until the age of 19, and it had managed to materialise.

Through that lens, as well as my unrivalled, sole love for those in the green and white hoops, I had never engulfed myself in the red and white of the Rosey Posey. So, how was I to create engaging content for a hoard of dedicated and devoted fans who were shut out of their club, when I was not one of them?

My concerns were quickly quashed, but not completely quashed when 'Big Brian' pulled the pearled account of John Allan's legendary status at the club out the bag. A sudden rush of pride, duty and comfort took over. Not to the degree of an episode of The Waltons, though. My mother would never allow that... yet.

Stemming a career

Throughout my time at university, lecturers and tutors (as well as the odd guest) would declare the importance of versatility. An "add as many strings to your bow as you can," kind of chat. Never one to disobey—in truth quite the opposite, I'm a prized people-pleaser—I aimed to be as adaptable as a rubber band.

Why stop at live streams when commentary could be added too? I was the 11-year-old football fanatic who dreamed of a career in sports journalism ever since the seed was planted in her head by a teacher, due to my love of English and thankfully, sport, but I never pictured herself holding the microphone behind the camera. I should have though, given I never shut-up and could provide running commentary over anything and everything...

In spite of my long-standing gift of the gab, I could produce nothing more than one, continuous, high-pitched, mirror-shattering screech when Lee Currie, a dead-ball specialist, dispatched a 'postage-stamp free kick' in the 89th minute against an uber-expensive East Kilbride side who many tipped to lift the Lowland League title that season.

It was a significant moment on the park. A poignant one on the makeshift gantry that could only be reached by climbing a shaky ladder. As the camera cut and the role of commentator ended, my co-commentator Seán and I showered in the beauty, relief and exuberance a fan possesses in those moments that only football can produce. We embraced each other like a pair of reunited long-distance pals. It was a cornerstone moment in our own friendship but also a pivotal point in our transition from employees to fans.

I came to the realisation that there will always be an element of this job that feels nothing like hardship. Watching 22 bodies have a kickabout on a grassy field isn't the most strenuous of occupations, and there will invariably be a sense of enjoyment. But from that game onwards, it seemed a cheek to even call doing anything Rose-related, "work". That notion was even stronger with the overwhelming privilege I felt even being allowed inside a football ground during those pandemic times.

With that privilege came the pressure to produce, and it was largely self-inflicted pressure. There was an acute awareness, rather habitually on my part, that I had no scope for error. Certainly, no room to be lacking in knowledge or slipping up on the simple stuff. I've always had the offside rule down to a tee. Well, pre-VAR days when it was a simpler game...

During high school I answered the "what do you want to do when you leave?" question, in its various forms, with "a sports journalist." I was greeted with a few "oohs and ahs", the odd bottom-lip pout and many "that's an unusual choice" responses. I knew I was not going to go through my career without the odd questioning. But I did wonder why it would be like that. My friends who replied with "a teacher," "a biologist" and even "an interior designer" received responses with a very different tone. It's all in the tone. As my very wise gran proclaims, "It's not what you say, it's how you say it." She's 'the boss' for a reason.

The shame of the game

When the fixtures are released, everyone has teams and dates that their eyes are drawn to. Rivalries and derbies, opening day and birthday weekend ties. The festive period is a cracker too. Who doesn't revel in ditching family to dash to the game or the pub on New Year's Day?

The 2021 edition of this fantastic footballing date again had its own spin on things with the reapplied restrictions in place. For Rose fans, they were missing out on a double whammy. The game was a twice rearranged Scottish Cup match with Bo'ness United on the road toward the oldest trophy in association football. The bare mention of the 'gong' sends warm and fuzzy feelings inside anyone who has the faintest link to the Cupa na h-Alba (or Scottish Cup).

Those are tricky emotions to convey via a Facebook live stream...

Having said that, the thing about a Facebook live stream is that anyone and everyone can let you know right there and then how they are feeling. You're inviting commentary right back to you. That's helpful at times. At others, not so much.

I was knee-deep in calling the game and Rose were well up, eventually running out 5-2 winners. As professional as we tried to be, we were in the role to develop, learn and importantly, have fun and enjoy ourselves. All boxes were being ticked until the comment, *"aw Amy, give us peace, this is why women shouldn't commentate"* came through in the second half.

It was a sucker punch that provoked self-questioning and confusion within me. I simply couldn't explain the meaning behind this observation. There were no glaring errors or mishaps. I was just there as a young female in a budding journalistic career. That was all. But that is all there needs to be to spark such sexist remarks.

Comments of the kind instigate the flight or fight response. You can either tackle the situation head on and stand up for yourself and what is right, or you can shrink into your shell and succumb to the bullies. The latter appeared easier, quieter and certainly less painful, but that would really hurt and burst the bubble of 11-year-old Amy, and annoy her too, because boy—was she stubborn!

I'm many things, but I am no Mike Tyson. Much more a lover than a fighter. Catch me ringside, not mucking about on the canvas. My role models though, Scottish sports journalistic legends such as Hazel Irvine and Ginny Clark, and even more recently Jane Lewis and Eilidh Barbour have found themselves in the proverbial ring, fighting their battles on their own. Me? I had a squad of decent young male counterparts who were executing 'right hooks' on my behalf. Standing up for my place in the game and shutting down anyone who dared to suggest that I belong elsewhere.

The tide has far from turned, but there is a new wave flowing. The male journalists emerging today have a far more inclusive outlook compared to their predecessors who are unfortunately still lingering around. Anyone who denies that is kidding themselves. One year ago, I produced a documentary investigating whether sexism was scuppered or sustained in Scottish football media. No prizes for guessing the outcome.

Conversations about such a serious and live problem must not be silenced. Instead they must be heralded, and preferably through a megaphone. But here is not the time or the place for that. That episode was one wilting petal in my otherwise blossoming Rose tenure. It's a club who created a red wall behind me when it occurred, and that has never shifted since. And thank God they started building, because otherwise, I may have missed out on the best bit...

A new blooming

The COVID season curtailed, again. Rose was well in the hunt for raucous celebrations at the end of the campaign, punching above their weight alongside teams who were more lavishly resourced when the plug was pulled. The loss of my voice post East Kilbride was well worth it...

Take two. An early season chastening loss to Civil Service Strollers failed to derail a relentless train steered by manager Robbie Horn. Rose was vehement in pursuit of professional status, never once falling into the safety net of excuses at their disposal given the disparity in resources between the Glaswegian juggernauts and the little Rosey Posey.

Lowland League was blitzed in a triumphant crusade, but Rose were more than a stretch away from the untouched terrain of the SPFL. Up first was a two-legged tie against the Highland League champions, Fraserburgh. The Broch were brushed to one breezy side without too many bruises. Now it was time for a bite at the big guns. Club 42—Cowdenbeath.

Same script, home and away. And in a case of déjà vu, Bonnyrigg Rose very much put on a show at home, racking up a healthy advantage to take over the Forth the following week. Cowden manager Maurice Ross later said the damage done to his side in EH19 was irreversible, and that their fate was sealed after the sobering 3–0 defeat in the first match. Football can be a funny old game, though…

Nevertheless, the narrative was etched in stone. Cowden's casket began lowering before a ball was kicked in front of the thousands of Rose fans who travelled through to Fife with formidable hope that the job would be completed. Among them were my Dad and brother.

While the boys settled their pre-match nerves—or got the shindig started early—in a local boozer, I took my place in the press box with a Rose badge on my chest for the final time. No matter what, my time with the club was coming to an end. My student life was ending and a leap into the big bad world was inevitably looming. I could no longer spend my time volunteering for the club I came to love so very much. I devotedly prayed that I'd be going out on a high.

Neil Martyniuk cut the coolest and calmest figure inside Central Park when he hovered over a spot kick that would ensure there was no coming back for Cowden. If it had not kicked off already, the party was in full swing now. Full swing, full circle. A bow tied on two special years at an exceptional club where I was allowed to leave my own mark with the following spiel as the final whistle blew in Fife.

"Bonnyrigg Rose have knocked and knocked and knocked on the previously closed door of the SPFL and now they follow in the footsteps of Edinburgh City, Cove Rangers and Kelty Hearts by becoming the latest club to beat through the pyramid system and become an SPFL club.

"Immortality will reign among this side. Undoubtedly, they go down with the Scottish Cup junior teams of 1966 and 1978. Today is a day to revel, today is a day to be proud of the Rosey Posey."

The rose in my side

Growing up, my friends loathed my fondness of football, never mind my newfound obsession. They were unable to grasp why I would turn down shopping days for standing in the freezing cold or how a game, or a result, would dictate my mood so profusely. But it did, it does and I reckon it forever will. Even more so now as I go through life with two great loves in the game.

I was a one-club girl. I did not need another. Celtic were the complete package. The highest of highs at home, the lowest of lows abroad. The less said about European ventures during the last 15 years, the better. But on a Scottish scale, I really was spoiled. What could I possibly be craving?

Football is family. I thought I knew that, but I know now I never truly felt and appreciated the meaning of it until Bonnyrigg Rose. Words fail to describe the spine-tingling feeling that surges through my skin when the cauldron of Celtic Park erupts, but the warmth in knowing everyone by name at New Dundas Park hits home differently, leaving me with no choice than to continue my affair and become a season-ticket holder.

It's a club that succeeds not because of their deep pockets, but because of the depth in soul, spirit and togetherness of the people at the crux of it.

Falling in love is not always easy, but there is a palpable pulse at Rose that makes it so. I have the bug and I can only imagine John Allan had the bug, too. Wherever he is, I hope he looks down on our rekindling with Rose with pride.

Amy Canavan is from Edinburgh in Scotland and graduated with a first-class honours degree in journalism in 2022. She has wanted to be a sports journalist since the idea was planted in her head by a primary school teacher. Amy says her voluntary work with Bonnyrigg Rose gave her the best two years in any role she has ever held, and that this story is "a love letter, a thank you and everything in between".

Three Goals That Changed Me

by Flora Snelson

Me vs University of South Wales, April 2019

On the nights before important games when I was playing football at university, I'd dip into my bank of former glories, replaying career highlights to feed my spirit in its most impressionable moments between wake and rest.

I don't know enough about consciousness, memory and bodies to know whether there's any causal link between striking a ball cleanly from the comfort of your duvet to bagging it at the moment it matters the following day, but if succeeding as a striker is a confidence game, then I'm sure as hell going to roll the dice on manifestation!

Whether or not I used this strategy on the night before scoring my goal against University of South Wales, I can't say—but whatever preparation I did set me up for a performance that will be on my mental showreel forever.

While everyone hopes their best playing days are still ahead of them, it wouldn't upset me to accept that the conclusion of the 2018/2019 season was my peak. Not having made the first team when I had been hopelessly frustrated and determined in my first year of university, I then grew three inches taller as captain of the second eleven in my second year, only to graduate to being a first team player during my final year at Bristol.

Also joining the first team then was new manager Bill, whose expectations, faith, discipline and fine footballing mind gave me more of an appetite for the sport than I had ever enjoyed—a fresh enthusiasm for a lifelong hobby.

As a team, we were extremely fit and together, spending four sessions a week playing football and a further three- to seven-hour stint drinking on

Wednesday nights. In another life, I'm a sport scientist studying the net benefit of those VK binges. I'm not sure whether what we gained in social cohesion makes up for what we lost in fitness—but in March 2019, with just a handful of games remaining, our league position indicated a strong vote in favour of such team bonding.

Though we were at the top of the tree, the University of South Wales (USW) had a reasonable shot at usurping us, and in the final stretch of the season we fought a six-pointer at their place.

The Welsh side had unbelievable facilities. Turning up to a FIFA-approved 3G pitch in the environs of what looked like a vast aerodrome, with its high ceiling and soft, echoey acoustics, only added to the occasion. In the dressing room, Bill dished out responsibilities, celebrating that we had central midfield maestro Ellie back 100% fit and calling on me to score some goals to settle the contest that could just about seal a place in the promotion play-offs.

For as long as I can remember, I have put pressure on myself to score goals, and remain susceptible to the toxic notion that absence from the scoresheet constitutes a failed endeavour. Striking the sweet spot between high standards/self-criticism and relaxing/patience is the foundation of good performance, so you might imagine that managers' and teammates' expectations would upset the balance—but knowing that Bill and I wanted the same thing was somehow a sharing of the burden.

In the cool but not quite fresh air of the indoor 3G pitch, I worked so hard that afternoon. I love scoring goals, but during the 2018/2019 season I loved leading a vicious press every bit as much. With hours of dedicated off-pitch work behind me, I had an engine and I was going to celebrate it by chasing down every half-chance and doing my best to frighten the goalkeeper, converting physicality into micro-psychological encroachments.

It's a beautiful thing, busting a lung. Maybe it pays off, maybe it doesn't, but with every extra ounce of painful effort you're tipping the scales of fortune slightly in the favour of your team—your friends, your colleagues.

Marginal gains edge squads onto podiums and trophies into clammy, grasping hands, but what burns brightest in my mind about this afternoon—the event which sometimes sends me drifting into a peaceful sleep—is a marriage of mastery and synchronicity.

I had nurtured faint and confusing affection for Annys ever since we snogged during my first term with the club. I had since fallen in love with and had my heart broken by one of her best friends. Annys was the fastest person on our team; she moved with elegance. We were friends (I think).

Only some of this mattered as I raced toward the USW box, watching Annys belt down the left wing with the ball at her feet, leaving some poor Welsh full-back for dust. At the by-line, without halting for breath, she whipped a cross that I met at the front post, using the outside of my boot to punch the ball across the keeper and into the back of the net!

Here, it's the wannabe journalist in me that's filling in the gaps in my fallible memory, trotting out established verbal routines to paint the pictures between what really remains in my mind—two vivid and sharp stills—Annys, poised to distribute the ball from the very edge of the pitch, and then the goalkeeper, frozen in a picture of desperation, hands splayed, the ball already well past her left shoulder. Everything I do on a football pitch that is worth remembering comes back to me this way—in detailed, dramatic frames like photographs.

If you dream of scoring the perfect goal, you might fantasise about the clattering of the crossbar caused by Tony Yeboah's long-range first-time volley; or see the world upside down like Wayne Rooney's washing-machine wonder-strike. But that day, I felt every bit as unstoppable for the sheer speed, instinct and collaboration of our very run-of-the-mill goal.

"Remember that goal we scored?" comes up still on the few occasions when Annys and I meet, our front-post run in Pontypridd becoming the very stuff of legend.

When we won the league weeks later, it was momentous. Before or since, I've never achieved so much with a bunch of people working so hard for each other. It's total joy and a beautiful lesson to learn.

Jack Marriott vs Leeds United, May 2019

Until I reached the age of 22, winning and losing as a fan was straightforward—it was good or it was bad, and there was nothing more to say. I remember the flat feeling of anger when Leeds United's promotion play-off dreams were spoiled by Watford in 2006, then bitter disappointment when Cristiano Ronaldo's Portugal knocked England out of the World Cup on penalties later that year. Looking back, both outcomes were deserved, but fairness doesn't matter to an eight-year-old mind—what mattered was that someone else got the thing that I wanted.

The hilarious thing about football is that many supporters carry this skewed sense of injustice with them all their lives, bearing eternal grudges against bent referees and swearing blindly that their team never gets what they truly deserve, like the fiercest of protective mothers.

By virtue of my Dad, I belonged to Leeds United from birth, and their fan base is no different from the rest. But of the lot, they've perhaps got one of the greatest chips on their shoulder—and maybe for good reason. Then blissfully ignorant of it in my infancy, the Whites were left to rack and ruin by starry-eyed mismanagement, so I was condemned to spend my childhood and adolescence bearing witness to a painful rebuild as the club scrambled to return to where they rightfully "deserved" to be.

On my annual visits to Elland Road with my Dad, fans around me who had clung on through the fall never let up in their vocal belief in the team's greatness, though our journeys back down the A1 after the final whistle were rarely buzzing in triumph. But it was OK—I'd had a nice day out with my Dad. In his Ford Focus we'd listen to the classified results and I would think how pleased Callum and Anna and Luke and the other 80% of my classmates who supported Manchester United or Chelsea would be when I saw them the next day.

Sometimes I wonder how my love of football sustained itself through childhood and adolescence, without the carrot of victory, glory and silverware—but it did. That changed when I was 21 years old, as the arrival of Argentina's Marcelo Bielsa at Elland Road transformed my relationship with Leeds United from dutiful, warm and cosy to gripping and electric.

I'm not alone. In West Yorkshire, the Argentine manager started a cultural revolution that will be written about for decades to come, turning water to wine on the pitch and shaping fans' ideas about love, fairness and endeavour through his press conferences that are either spare or loquacious, and enigmatic or candid.

This was my reward—I'd waited, uninspired, through years of mediocrity, bound by loyalty to a club I had adopted by default, only to come of age and see the world of football brought alive by a stranger. After 16 years in exile from the top-flight league, the hopes of the Elland Road faithful were faltering and near-lifeless on the floor before Bielsa grabbed them by the scruff of the neck and promised triumph. With Leeds on track for promotion as the 2018/2019 season drew to a close, for the first time in my life as a fan, I had something to lose—results became excruciating.

Despite having progressed from naive little dot in her dad's white, yellow and blue scarf to a card-carrying voyeur of the Whites' ugly Twitter community, where opinions are thrown around like balls of dung, I could do no more about the slipping of Leeds' once-infallible promotion charge than I could prevent the team's outclassing by Watford and Portugal years previously. But what separated those helpless senses of desperation is that my grown-up, sophisticated understanding of the game had given me a sure belief that this time, what was happening before my eyes was plainly wrong.

Where was the fairy-tale ending Leeds deserved?

After feeling sure we'd storm the castle and hoist the flag with relatively little trouble, I think I was content to settle for a dramatic climax to the season; instead of cruising into the Premier League with a series of routine results. Perhaps Bielsa's footballing rebellion deserved a bloodthirsty ending no less than seizing victory from the jaws of defeat with a play-off final win at Wembley, the home of football—the ultimate flag in the ultimate ground.

After United limped to the end of the Championship season with three losses and a draw, their tidy 1-0 win in the first leg of the semi-final against Derby County seemed to promise the 'resumption of normal service'. For what was set to be a magnificent occasion, I went with two of my fondest friends from my university football team to watch the second leg at the Open Arms in Bristol. It was my way of introducing Jess and Elena, supporters of Liverpool and Everton respectively, to what they could expect from Leeds in the Premier League the following season. It was a sneak preview of sorts, and a chance to finally share my love of the team that was hardly important enough to make it onto television broadcasts up until then. As much as to support me, my friends were also there for their own entertainment since Bielsa's 'shit-or-bust' Leeds always guaranteed a fun watch.

That day, it was bust. It's easy to say that as soon as things started to go wrong, the expiry of the Whites' all-too-comfortable two-goal cushion was inevitable, but that steadfast belief in justice and deserving meant I clung to hope with every atom of my being until the bitter end. In retrospect, it all seems painfully obvious, Jack Marriott's winning goal for Derby was just a grim detail.

Life, as it rumbles on day after day after day, causes the constant revision of our perception of the past. Now for instance, Gareth Southgate's final-hurdle fall at Wembley with the English men's team in the delayed Euro 2020 feels nothing more to me than a helpful pre-cursor to the Lionesses' ultimate Euro success the following year. I now perceive it as whetting my appetite—though I know in the moment it hurt deeply.

Likewise, can the magnificence of Bielsa's subsequent promotion triumph discharge the Whites' 2019 play-off failure of all its spiky despair?

Then, for a short while in 2022, the imminent threat of relegation from the Premier League stripped the memory of fighting and praying to get there of all its meaning, making me feel as silly as someone who loses sleep over a jigsaw that you'll only break up again moments after completion.

Taking that approach, the pain of Marriott's goal to send Derby County through to the play-off final instead of Leeds United is confined to the past. In sport, emotion and consequence are intimately bound—just as glory is temporary, so is heartbreak—you'll play again next Saturday or next season, or when the next four-year cycle elapses, and your hopes will be raised again.

Chloe Kelly vs Germany, July 2022

"Don't look at the pictures just yet—when you do, the experience ends and it becomes a memory," was the advice Elena gave me as I reached for my phone on the Tube home from Wembley Stadium on July 31, 2022.

The carriage was calm, since my best friend and I had missed the mad underground bottleneck by staying so long after the final whistle, desperate to drink it all in. With our feet up on the seats, our cheeks flush with energy and joy, her advice helped preserve the most special day of my life for just a little longer.

What did the Lionesses' Euro win mean? It's tough to put into words—when I revisit the final, seeing footage and pictures from a distance of some months, I'm struck by the unique feeling it gives me.

All my life I've experienced the thrill of winning, the idolisation of players and the power of feeling part of something on the terraces—but England's triumph maximised all of these blessings and added a little more wonder besides. It is the closest thing to a "dream" I have experienced in my waking hours—a moment characterised by disbelief, euphoria and a queer, overwhelming sense of countless vital threads coming together at just the right time. Today, my heart swells with the memory.

What did the Lionesses' Euro win mean? Why did it matter? As Leah

Williamson subsequently put it, the legacy of the tournament wasn't about winning. Chloe Kelly's close-range toe-poke was not THE moment when the Lionesses' changed women's football in England forever and put the sport in front of new eyes—the entire Euro event created carnivals in towns like Rotherham and Wigan and brought kids to their feet with moments of drama and exhibitions of skill.

Lucy Bronze was on Pepsi bottles and Gary Lineker was tweeting about the event. I nearly dropped my pint when I discovered that the pub was showing a group stage game while I was holidaying in Ilfracombe, Devon. And then, there was Alessia Russo. Why did that goal matter? Well, Kelly brought it home but Russo made women's football seriously cool. It was audacious, it was skilful, it was playful, it was football at its finest—thinking outside the box and being creative.

She later explained that in the moment, she simply chose the quickest route to goal. Somehow, she found a way to put the ball in the onion bag, and she became a viral spectacle in the process. England reaching the final was the fairy-tale moment I always believed we would get, but that second half at Bramall Lane gave me butterflies.

Is this it? I asked myself. *Is something really enormous about to happen?*

The final is the only event in my life that prompts me to declare, unapologetically and emphatically, that it was truly like all of my birthdays and Christmases coming at once!

I attended with my parents, my sisters and Elena, (who I'd met playing football at university and with whom I had since become as thick as thieves). The night before the big day, I stayed at her place in Notting Hill, and she and I spent the evening traipsing around West London in pursuit of Panini stickers to mark the occasion.

Months later in December, I met a friend of a friend for the first time in a pub. Making conversation, I asked her if she was interested in football, and she said, "not really because it's pointless".

"And that's why it's beautiful," was my response.

Football's pointlessness is never more pointed than in the lead-up to a make-or-break fixture. Your body is consumed with emotions—dread, nerves, excitement, hope and fear—feelings you might associate with funerals, exams, weddings and childbirth, yet none of the ball-kicking will ever materially impact your life. It's feelings for fun, it's walking to a cliff's edge just for the hell of it.

And so I bubbled with exhilaration on the morning of the Euro 2022 final. But when we reached Baker Street to change onto the Metropolitan line for Wembley Park, the thrill shifted. Suddenly I wasn't just a wound-up jack-in-the-box primed to go off at the mere sight of Jill Scott's unmistakable stature from the distance of our seats up with the gods—no, when we changed at Baker Street I became a tiny, happy fish in a huge shoal of people who, liked me, loved women's football.

It was a feeling totally separate from the camaraderie I'd experienced at the heart of the Elland Road south stand. The fans on the Tube were 'my people' in a way that no Leeds United supporter had ever been—and it had nothing to do with where we were from.

There's a picture from England's Group A tie against Northern Ireland that explains it. In the foreground, Leah Williamson fixes her ponytail, while, out of focus and facing the other way, Keira Walsh is adjusting her headband in almost perfect symmetry. On finding this photo, I felt peace tinged with sadness, having reached the age of 25 before fully understanding what people meant when they talked about their footballing heroes.

Yes, I learnt from Didier Drogba and I'll admire Kalvin Phillips to the day I die. But seeing the captain of the England team securing her hair mid-match, her face fixed with focus—it reminded me of me, as a young girl, tucking fly-aways behind my ears and holding my breath for kick-off.

Williamson's ponytail and the Metropolitan line made me feel a part of something in a way that I never had before. At the other end of that transformative Tube ride, Wembley was waiting, but so too was a moment of serendipity that puts all of this nebulous sentimentality into focus. As I climbed the steps away from the platform at Wembley Park, I recognised another ponytail—I think?

I paused for a couple of seconds, checking myself, and then I didn't wait for the emergence of Jill Scott from the tunnel. I just went off there and then in the midst of a heavy crowd, with all of my buzz coming to a head in a series of shouts—"POLLY! POLLY! POLLY!"

Polly was the first team's number 1 when I joined the University of Bristol Women's Football Club in 2016. She still has a navy Umbro hoodie of mine that I leant her on an impossibly cold match day probably somewhere in Wales, though I didn't mention that on Wembley Way, when seeing her again for the first time in years.

"Sophie's up ahead," she told me, and there Sophie was too, and as I'm hugging Sophie, I spot Annys, and as I'm shouting "HELLO!" in Annys' face, Ash and Kelsey hove into view. By this point, I was practically frothing at the mouth.

It was kick-off minus approximately 40 minutes of the most important football game of my life and by chance I'd bumped into a bunch of the girls who shared my most precious memories of playing. Except it wasn't chance. It was destined to be. The coming together of tens and thousands of the country's most dedicated and excited female football fans—down the years, I'd probably played with or against tens more in that Wembley crowd. It was just that July 31 had been the first unofficial national conference of this community.

Football has given and will continue to give me so many friends in life, and Kelly's winning goal in extra time started the ultimate party among a sea of people drawn to each other by a shared love.

So, what *did* the Lionesses' Euro win mean? England's legacy is winning, but also love.

Their historic trophy lift rested on talent and confidence earned through years and years of nurturing a tiny flame—catalysed of course by a little bit of Sarina Wiegman genius. The tournament caused my own flame to roar brighter, while lighting one afresh in the hearts of thousands of young girls.

Flora Snelson is a football writer and player from Cambridge, UK. After penning plays and pantomimes while studying English at university, she began writing about her beloved Leeds United. This led her to a stint covering the mighty Whites at the Yorkshire Evening Post. Now, she is part of The Square Ball team who make podcasts and magazines for Leeds United fans. Sign-up to Flora's weekly newsletter on the women's game, 31/7, by going to www.thesquareball.net/31-7.

Football. Bloody Hell.

by Steffany Wangari Ndei

The origin of my villain story

The only reason I went unnoticed while watching the 2008 African Cup of Nations (AFCON) semi-final between Ghana and Egypt was that my father and his brothers were deeply engrossed in conversation about politics in the country. On a normal day, I would have been asked to change the TV station to the 9pm news and shooed away to go help the maid clean up the dinner dishes.

I was lucky that a football match was even showing because no one in that household really cared about the game. It was only showing because the commentary was a sensible backdrop to the critical discussion going on among the adults in the room. Football was such a rare sight in the room that that match was the first game I had ever watched at 14 years old, despite being obsessed with the sport years before then.

My interest in football had gone surprisingly unnoticed by my parents—they had no interest in football at all even though they were interested in me. I was doing well in school despite experiencing the typical discipline problems any "tomboy" girl does, like fighting with boys.

Had my father known the impact this AFCON semi-final game had on me, he probably would have chosen Cartoon Network to play during the discussion. Ironically, despite being so nonchalant about football, he had been to the World Cup in 2002 as the leader of the Boy Scouts in Kenya. He came back with a football as a gift to my brother—but I was the one who enjoyed it more, kicking the ball against the wall when none of my neighbours was up for a kickabout.

Thanks to the football grapevine at school where lads would debate all matches from the English Premier League (EPL) to the AFCON with the punditry prowess of Gary Lineker and Gary Neville, I knew who to watch out for in the match. Junior Agogo. In hindsight, even if I hadn't had any idea who to root for, I would still have chosen Agogo's team because by my 14-year-old standards, I found him to be one hell of a gorgeous human being!

After the match, I was keen to join the boys at school to discuss the game and hone my debating and oratory skills, and to swear by Agogo's name that Ghana deserved to win (though I would not disclose my attraction to him). However, that idea didn't go to plan. According to them, I had no business discussing football with boys and there was no way I would say anything sensible. Everything I said or tried saying was ignored—just like my father and his brothers ignored the game that has shaped my life.

The Ghana vs Egypt game awakened all sorts of fires in me. As much as I wanted to be heard during football discussions, I yearned to corner people like Agogo and take them on. I wanted to be part of a team. The only place I could possibly play with anyone was in school with the boys who had 'bugged me off' from their punditry discussions.

I caved to my temptations one day and asked to join them.

I was sure I wouldn't be the worst on the pitch, and even if I were, I would have fun while I was playing. They played with a paper ball and I asked the most popular lad if I could join. He was popular, thankfully because he was the smartest in class and not because he was a bully.

"You want to play? Are you sure?"

"Yep!"

"Well, join Benjamin's team," he said.

There was no time to learn who my teammates were. I knew Benjamin but I didn't know his teammates (there was no way to figure that out anyway because everyone on both teams played in their school uniforms). Break time was only 30 minutes and the whole field was full of kids (mostly boys) chasing paper balls. It was like every class had a paper ball and incredible that 20 games of football were being played on the field at the same time!

"Benjamin, I am on your team, Timo has told me to play for your team!" I yelled to Benjamin who was concentrating on the game, trying not to lose sight of the paper ball affiliated with our class.

"OK, you will be the goalkeeper," Benjamin said. "I was goalkeeper, but I'll be the last man."

Any role would do—I just wanted to play. Soon, we were defending my goal line. It turned out that Timo had put me on the weak team and Benjamin, who was always deployed as the goalkeeper because he was the fat kid, had found someone to relieve him of his fat-kid duties.

The ball was kicked toward me and my teammates yelled at me to catch it with my hand since I was the goalkeeper. Word had travelled fast that I was the new 'signing'. I had a long dress on and so had an advantage as a goalkeeper. I could stretch my legs and the ball wouldn't be able to go between them. In essence, nutmegging me was impossible. However, I didn't handle the ball with my hands. I dribbled it past two opponents and kicked it downfield.

"How can a girl dribble past you?" yelled one of Timo's teammates.

Benjamin was clapping his hands. I was staying true to my mission of not being the worst on the pitch and having fun while playing.

The game ended goalless. After break time, the lads talked about my performance and Timo gave a talking down to his teammates for "letting a girl" dribble past them and not scoring against me. Others said I only got lucky because I had a dress on. Benjamin and my mates, happy that we did not concede, didn't care how we got a draw against the team that apparently beat them day in and day out. If wearing a dress was the recipe for 'shithousery', so be it, but it didn't justify that they drew with a team that had a girl!

Since that day, I have worn shorts under my dress and changed during break time because I didn't want to give anyone the satisfaction of thinking that my dress gave me 'superpowers'. I had the same colour shorts as the lads, just in case a teacher decided to inspect the field of play in search of a truant, football-obsessed girl. I also had short hair, but in retrospect I was overly careful not to be noticed since no teacher would spot me on a field with 20 paper balls and kids of all ages going berserk.

School finally had meaning. I dreaded the national exams that determined which high school I would be deployed to and I changed my ambitions—much to my father's dismay—from being an astronaut to being a footballer. I simply wanted to play.

At home, I found an alliance of kids who were football-mad. I had found my tribe and we found an open space in between buildings to play in. We named it "Anfield" because there was already a "Wembley" in a different neighbourhood. My interest in football was no longer because of circumstances such as my Dad bringing home a football gift for my brother, or because I loved listening to boys debate about the best goal of the weekend in school. It was because I chose to play football and I was, apparently, very good at it!

"As long as you give me my grades, you can play your football"

It was in high school that my football obsession got my parents riled up. I was in an all-girls boarding school. My parents had hoped I would outgrow my liking for the sport and that I would at least start "behaving like a girl". Even though I was in a private school where my schoolmates chose to keep their nails long instead of playing a game, I still found time to play. Being the team's captain did not do much to douse my obsession. I had access to where the balls were stored and I could, as I often did, get the ball and play like I did at home—kicking a ball against the wall.

Because I had no discipline problems and I played at the appropriate time, the teachers let me do it. During important fixtures such as the 2010 World Cup final, I was also allowed to watch the game with other teachers in the dining hall. However, back at home, the rift with my parents because of my obsession with football was haunting me.

While I looked forward to school holidays (because it meant I didn't have to wake up at 5am, stick to tasteless diets, wear the same clothes and adhere to mundane routines), I loathed being home for the holidays because it meant I couldn't watch or play football. My father made the 'laws', saying I was not allowed to go out and play football and my mother was 'the court', enforcing the law and beating me up whenever I erred.

Even though I was recognised as the best footballer in school at the annual prize-giving ceremony, my parents wished I was honoured for my brains rather than my brawn. In form three, just one year before the final high school national exams (which would determine the course I would study at university and whether I would qualify for a government scholarship), my grades took a hit. Because of that, I was suspended from school and asked to return with my father.

"Why are your grades not reflecting your potential, Steffany?" asked Mr Alex, the school principal.

I was not 'home' at home. I felt like an outcast whenever I was there because even though I could play football at school, it was never like playing football with my chosen tribe at "Anfield".

"It's because of my Dad," I said.

"What do you mean?" Mr Alex probed.

"He won't let me play football," I said.

Mr Alex chuckled. My father was silent, perhaps out of embarrassment more than concern.

"If he lets you play, will your grades improve?" Mr Alex asked.

"Yes, it's not that I play during class. I play when I don't have class scheduled or when I have finished all my assignments," I replied.

"Well, is that all you want?" my father interrupted.

I nodded in affirmation. I still couldn't look him in the eye.

"Well, as long as you give me my grades, you can play your football," he said.

I wanted to say, "say no more, Dad". But I figured I would rather put my money where my mouth was. From that day, a silent pact was signed with my father. I could play football as long as I did well in school.

I passed the national exams, getting a grade that earned me a government scholarship to university to study sociology. I was 18 and felt that I had paid my dues with my parents. I had little interest in a university education as I had my sights set on a career in professional football.

Little did I know that boarding school and a shelter at home had shielded me from the harsh realities of playing football in Kenya—or any other place in the world really, especially as a woman.

"Just how good is she?"

There was a new regime at the helm of Kenya's democracy. Much as their victory in the ballot was controversial because of the crimes against humanity charges they faced at the International Criminal Court at The Hague, Kenyans felt they had 'flipped off' the West by electing the very candidates the West advised against. The regime under Uhuru Kenyatta and William Ruto hit the ground running. One of their programs was to set up a National Youth Talent Academy, which benefitted me.

There was a try-out in all 47 counties in Kenya and I was selected for the football academy after successfully impressing the scouts in my home county, Machakos. Fresh from high school, I knew this was the right path to follow if I wanted to play for the women's national team.

At the academy, I was with kids about my age and younger who had all been selected from the try-outs. I went back to my high school routine—waking up early, sticking to a timed eating schedule, but unlike school where I had to endure physics lessons, I was going through football drills. I loved it! If this was what I had to go through to be as big as Ronaldo, I was going to give my all.

Even though I was the stand-out athlete in high school and in my hometown, the academy opened my eyes to a different world of girls who were disgustingly good. I knew right away that I had work cut out for myself, not just because I was tiny in stature, but because kicking a ball against the wall didn't help my tactical understanding of the game. What's more, most of my mates at the academy came from a lower social class and were there not just because they were good at football, but also because they had no other means of raising their social status. To them, football was not just the means but the end. They had backing from their parents to play football because they had seen players like Dennis Oliech and Mike Origi (Divock Origi's father) climb out of the slums because of the game.

And so we played. On the pitch, the only thing that separated us was our skills and knowledge of the game. I didn't want them to think I was a pushover—a kid who bribed their way into the academy. And I knew the proletarian revolution would manifest in that setting—a perception that as a kid who had gone to a private school, I had no business dominating their territory.

We earned (or were supposed to earn) a monthly allowance of 3000 Kenyan shillings. At the time, it was equivalent to USD30. The academy honoured the allowance for the first month but we earned nothing in the next two. It was meant to be a three-month excursion and so in the final two months, the coaches—who were also victims of the unpaid allowance—stopped showing up. We also had no food at the academy and we only stayed because we had the Copa Coca-Cola tournament to honour. It was during that tournament that my father got a glimpse of my talent. Or heard about it.

There were scouts at each phase of the tournament—the lowest being the zonal stage and the highest being the national stage—who selected the best players to advance to the national stage. Thanks to the pool of talent we had at the academy, most of us advanced to the next stages without any struggle. We dominated every match we played. It was at the provincial stage, the level just before the national stage, that we lost some of my teammates. But I was selected to represent my province on the national stage alongside the kids who had played ball in the same slums of Nairobi that have nurtured Kenya's greats, such as McDonald Mariga and Victor Wanyama. It was such a huge feat that when my Dad received the call about my selection, he asked: "Just how talented is she?"

The top performers on the national stage were called up to the national team. Even though I didn't make it, the Copa Coca-Cola tournament opened doors for me to play for clubs in Nairobi. My hometown was Machakos, 54 km from the capital of Nairobi. Any serious football—let alone women's football—was played in Nairobi, and I understood that convincing my parents to let me play football in Nairobi would be tough. The only way I would step foot in Nairobi, unsupervised, would be if I was going to school.

"This football thing"

My mother, while still enforcing the rules of my father, had softened her heart to my exploits. Thanks to having a shop in Machakos town where most footballers and football fans went, she had heard of my prowess. Most of them convinced her to feed me, saying I was really good but very skinny. She also bore most of the brunt when I came home dirty, spent or injured. She became so accustomed to it that she could tell when I was coming from a game we had lost. It was emotionally taxing for her to listen to me vent about unpaid allowances and how a coach taunted me for playing for another team (even when I was not contractually bound to play for a specific club).

"What do you think you can make out of this football, Wangari?" she asked, one day.

"I want to play in Europe or the USA," I said.

"And then what? Where will this football take you?"

"I don't know Mum, people become coaches when they retire. I could be like Sir Alex Ferguson."

She didn't know who Sir Alex Ferguson was but she knew I was deluded to think I could make a living out of football. To her, football brought out the worst in me, because I always complained about how there was dishonour among coaches and players, and that it made me so skinny people thought she didn't feed me. It was also making me crude as I had become rash to my siblings, like players always are to referees. It was, if anything, making me uncultured.

I yearned every day to get a breakthrough to play abroad. I signed up for academies that played their tournaments in Scandinavian countries but I could not keep up with the commuting demands from Machakos to Nairobi to honour the training sessions or the matches. But after hearing enough about my heroics and enduring my groans and moans about football in Nairobi or Machakos, my mother decided to help me find a way out of the rogue football situation in Kenya and asked a relative to apply for me to go to college in the US.

I was admitted but the tuition fees were so expensive that my parents had to fundraise to pay for the first semester. The goal was to have me try out for colleges that would give me a scholarship. I tried out for Grand View University in Iowa and earned a half-scholarship.

I was en route to being the biggest star in women's football, if not in the world, at least in Kenya!

But something happened to my psyche while I was playing in Iowa. At the peak of my football career, I felt empty. It felt like I was burnt out from trying too hard in Kenya. I had foregone the government scholarship there, and my college mates were now graduating with their bachelor's degrees. I was 23 years old, the oldest in my college team, and here I was, chasing a dream. Unlike the kids I played with in Machakos or Nairobi, my teammates in the US were just playing football for the sake of playing. None had grand dreams of becoming the next Messi. Few cared about European football and their priorities were miles different from mine. The existential crisis of being in the land of opportunity with no end in sight for my struggles created a dissonance so great that I lost the purpose of playing football.

The presence of mind I had when I realised that the kids at the academy played football because it was their 'bread and butter' occurred to me again, and I remembered my mother's words: "What will this *football* thing help you with?"

I played with and against the best footballers in my life in the US. But the fact they were not professional footballers got to me. What was worse, I could only think of two women footballers who had made a successful career from Kenya.

What if I don't make it? Heck, do I even want to make it? Do I want to be a professional footballer? I questioned myself.

The questions didn't stop there. *Why did I have to travel miles away from home to realise this dream? Why can't I achieve it in Kenya? And why are the kids who only have football to save them from damnation damned to live in Kenya? Can I make a difference by being a footballer? How?*

If anything, my life in Iowa brought out the philosopher in me.

I remembered too that it wasn't football that had got me there. Perhaps my parents were right. Perhaps "this *football* thing" was a waste of my time. Were it not for my grades in high school, I would not have been admitted to a university in Iowa. If anything, my exploits in school had opened more doors for me than "this *football* thing".

After one season, I went to my head coach's office and told him I was going back to Kenya. I had talked to my parents about my decision and it might have felt like their prayers were answered; that my football demons had been exorcised and I was finally back to my senses.

"I just want to study," I told Ventsi, my coach.

"You know, how Americans approach football is different from your culture and where I come from," Ventsi said. "If you were on the boys' team, your experience would be different because they have players from Europe."

He was right, the little reverence that Americans have for soccer had played a part in my falling out of love with the game, but there was a much bigger issue at play; what was "this *football* thing" going to do for me after all the sacrifices I had made?

Ventsi tried convincing me to stay. He called a different college who offered me a full scholarship and gave me some time to change my mind. But the support from my parents strengthened my resolve. I booked my flight to Kenya, said goodbye to my teammates and swore never to kick another ball in my life when I went back home.

Food for my soul

Two weeks after I arrived back in Kenya, I went to the local playground in Machakos. The kids in high school who only played during the school holidays had graduated, which meant they played every day throughout the year. They had formed a team, Machakos Youth, and had practice sessions every day of the week.

I watched them as they were playing "el rondo" on the red soil with all the mirth and joy of the most innocent kids in Africa who believe they will be like Sadio Mané. I wept. It was not the regret that I had squandered a life-changing opportunity that weighed on my heart. It was the realisation that the odds of them making it were against them, yet they still believed with all their hearts that they too could be like Victor Wanyama.

After a month of being a mere onlooker, I found myself back on the pitch—this time not only playing, but also coaching the lads. I knew telling them to give up on their dreams because the statistics were against them would yield nothing. From the experience with my parents, no one exorcises that demon out of you. You exorcise it yourself by living through it.

We created an unbeatable team in Machakos. I coached them while diligently going to university. I transferred my credits from Iowa and enrolled in journalism school. I had swapped priorities but decided that it was unrealistic to think that I would never play professional football.

I learnt to avoid answering questions about what happened in the US and why I came back with nothing to show for it. I turned down offers to play in the Kenyan Women's Premier League and only played five-a-side tournaments. It only played with Machakos Youth.

I was mentally in the pits after coming back. Heck, if I'm being honest, I was mentally unwell when I made the decision to stop playing college football. And so going back home to a country that has very little to offer its burgeoning youth only made things worse. Yes, I went to class every day, and played football when I could, but I was empty inside and had no will to live.

What kept me alive was my time with Machakos Youth. I looked forward to watching them play, coaching them and playing with them. Most of the lads in that team only had football to save them from a life of crime and addiction. In retrospect, I also only had football to save me. "This *football* thing" was literally saving my life and keeping suicidal thoughts at bay.

I kept my head down and let go of the possibilities of football replenishing my coffers. It was no longer just a means—it was an end—and food for my soul.

I still play occasionally and, like Drake raps, "I still love it but I used to love it more."

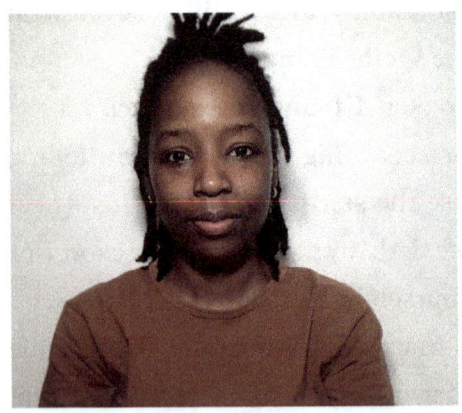

Steffany Wangari Ndei from Kenya is a graduate student currently pursuing a master of arts in sports ethics and integrity. She aims to become an investigative sports journalist with a focus on shedding light on ethical issues within African football.

The Judging Panel

Marcela Mora y Araujo (Argentina) is a freelance journalist who has been exploring football as art, culture, and business since 1991. She has written and broadcast for a wide range of outlets including the BBC, talkSPORT, The Economist, The Financial Times, The Guardian, Olé, La Nación, Four Four Two and Cambio 16 to name a few. She has also written extensively on football related violence, international transfer markets, and issues of national identity for numerous specialist academic, human rights, and arts journals.

She is the author of *Ossie's Dream* (2010) the autobiography of Ossie Ardiles; is the official English translator of Diego Maradona's autobiography *El Diego* (2000), and author of a digital essay on Carlos Tevez for Random House (2014).

Marcela has won prizes for television documentaries, and she has also been awarded prizes by the International Sports Press Association (AIPS) awards in 2022 and 2023.

She is one of the few living journalists to have interviewed the Argentina trinity of Alfredo Di Stéfano, Maradona and Lionel Messi.

Stephanie Brantz (Australia) is an experienced journalist, broadcaster and MC who has worked with SBS, the Nine Network, the ABC, ESPN and SEN Radio.

She is Chair of the Sports Diplomacy Advocacy Network of the Australian Department of Foreign Affairs and Trade, and is also a Board member of Football NSW and the Sydney Cricket Ground Trust.

Nick Harris (Scotland) is an award-winning investigative journalist who has worked in the UK, France, Kenya and Japan, specialising in the business and finance of sport, notably football, and football corruption, doping, supporter issues across all sports and the growing relationship between sport, money, geopolitics, and power. He is the author of the Global Sports Salaries Survey.

Major scoops include breaking the Russia state-doping story months before the Sochi Games, and the subsequent impact on Russia 2018 (or lack of impact); breaking FIFA corruption stories that led to prosecutions and in some cases dismissals within hours of publication, including that of Sepp Blatter's No 2 Jerome Valcke; and revealing how Britain's anti-doping agency let British Cycling effectively police themselves in the run-up to London 2012, an investigation that led to UKAD being censured by WADA.

He is co-author of *A Man in a Hurry – The Extraordinary Life and Times of Edward Payson Weston, the World's Greatest Walker* (2012).

PERSONAL STORIES

Inas Mazhar (Egypt) is the Managing Editor of Al Ahram Weekly and Head of Sport for Al Ahram - the first woman to head the sports section of a major newspaper in Egypt. She is also the only woman among 100 jury members for France Football magazine's prestigious Ballon d'Or award.

She is an Adjunct Professor of Sports Media at the University of Cairo, a member of the Women and Sport Committee of the Egyptian Olympic Committee, a member of the Egyptian Handball Commission, and the International Sports Press Association.

Inas has also worked as media officer and Media Director for CAF and FIFA events.

Bonita Mersiades (Australia) is the founder of Fair Play Publishing, the Football Writers' Festival, and the Emerging Women Writers' program. She has worked voluntarily and professionally in football, including as team manager of the Socceroos and Head of Corporate and Public Affairs for Football Australia, prior to which she worked in government and the non-profit health sectors.

Bonita is recognised internationally as a FIFA whistleblower who called-out FIFA for corruption and questionable business practices prior to the FIFA arrests in May 2015. She has written and presented extensively on football issues for organisations and publications in UK, Europe, North and South America and Asia. She has twice presented to the European Parliament on football governance and corruption issues advocating for, inter alia, a world sport anti-corruption agency.

She is the author of *My World Is Round,* the playing biography of Frank Farina (1998); *Whatever It Takes - the Inside Story of the FIFA Way* (2018) - the only book written by an insider on the corrupt 2018/2022 World Cup bidding process and which has been the subject of documentaries in Germany, Switzerland, the UK and the USA - and *Portraits in Football* (2022).

Osasu Obayiuwana (Nigeria) a British-Nigerian lawyer, has been reporting on African and world football, as well as its politics and governance issues, for over 25 years.

Osasu has been a writer and broadcaster with the BBC's Sport Interactive, television and World Services as a staff and freelance reporter, particularly for the World Football programme. A weekly offering which is coming to an end in March 2023. He periodically writes on international football for the The Guardian and the London Observer, as well The Blizzard.

He served on FIFA's defunct anti-racism task force for three years (2013-2016) and has also advised the Nigerian Football Federation on governance reform. Osasu was also a part of a team of lawyers that prepared a legal roadmap on the establishment of a Nigerian Court of Arbitration for Sport, for the Nigerian Olympic Committee.

Laura Williamson (England) is deputy editor of The Athletic UK, with a dedicated responsibility for football news.

Previously, she spent 11 years at The Daily Mail, progressing from a football reporter to athletics correspondent and columnist before becoming sports news editor and then executive sports news editor.

Laura began her career in tennis and cricket working for Hawk-Eye Innovations.

MORE REALLY GOOD FOOTBALL BOOKS FROM FAIR PLAY PUBLISHING

The First Matildas

Encyclopedia of Matildas

Socceroos – A World Cup Odyssey

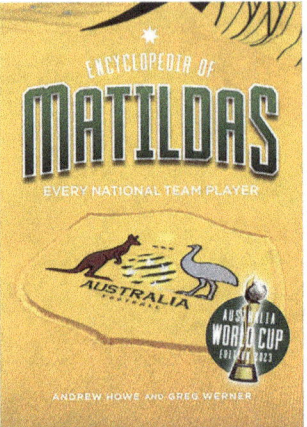
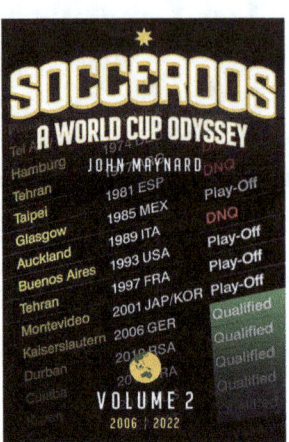

When Mum and Dad See Me Kick

Green and Golden Boots

"Get Your Tits Out for the Lads"

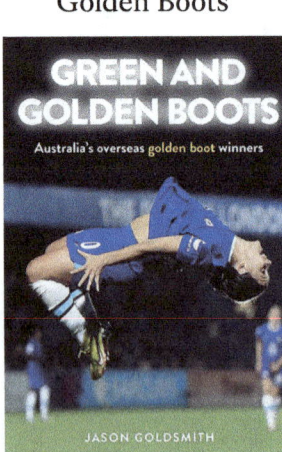

MORE REALLY GOOD FOOTBALL FICTION FROM POPCORN PRESS

Lucy Zeezou's Goal

Lucy Zeezou's Glamour Game

Anna Black – this girl can play

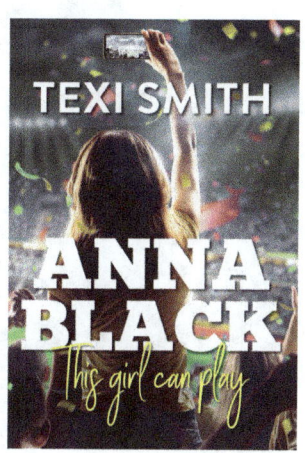

Game

The Gaffer

Jarrod Black Chasing Pack

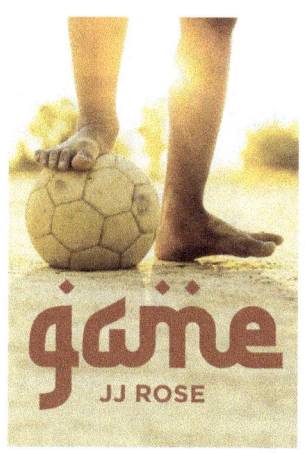

www.ingramcontent.com/pod-product-compliance
Lightning Source LLC
Chambersburg PA
CBHW072050110526
44590CB00018B/3117